School Administration, Supervision and Organisation

School Administration, Supervision and Organisation

Dr. Jagannath Mohanty

SHIPRA

ISBN: 978-81-7541-559-1

2014 Impression
First Published in 2011

School Administration, Supervision and Organisation

Published by:
SHIPRA PUBLICATIONS
H.O.: LG 18-19, Pankaj Central Market, I.P. Ext.,
Patparganj, Delhi 110092, Ph. 22235152, 22236152
Br. Off.: Ansari Road, Daryaganj,
New Delhi 110002; Ph.9650028065, 9810522367
Email: info@shiprapublications.com
Website: www.shiprapublications.com

PREFACE

The present book, designed for students of education, covers wide areas of school administration, supervision and organization. The original manuscript was prepared without the coverage of school organization but now three chapters have been added in this book keeping in view the requirement of curriculum as on date. The language of the book is simple and easy to understand. It is hoped pre and in-service teachers shall make the best use of the book. The author thanks the authors and their publishers for referring their works to enhance the value of the book for the benefit of students.

Prof. Jagannath Mohanty
Former Professor of Education,
Principal of Institute of Advance
Study in Education and Director,
Academic Staff College,
Utkal University.

CONTENTS

1

Meaning, Nature, Scope and Objectives of School Administration, Inspection and Supervision

(A) What is Inspection

Inspection means critical examination of one or more aspects of the school and its programmes. Historically speaking it was introduced in the educational system to enforce control and authority as an executive arm of the government. The officers in-charge of inspection were mainly administrative officials, who used to pay visit to schools with a view to checking the work of teachers and progress of pupils as per the rules and standards prescribed by the government from time to time. This was the original function of an inspector whatever may be the nomenclature in any country of the world. In England and India, where schools were given financial assistance or grants, it was the responsibility of the inspector to make assessment of the functions of teachers and standards of teaching for payment of grants to concerned schools. As a corollary to such activity inspection assumed a police character and an autocratic spirit. The relation between teachers and inspectors was not friendly, but, authoritarian; not based on cordial fellowship, but on hostile fear and suspicion.

The International Bureau of Education in one of its reports entitled "School Inspection" has given a comparative picture of inspection prevalent in sixty-six countries. The report aims at providing information mainly on inspection of primary education and to a lesser degree of secondary education and vocational education. The analysis of the data revealed that the majority of the 66 countries had special staff for inspecting primary schools. The designations of these staff members were usually inspectors. In a few countries they were, however, called counsellors, superintendents or supervisors. It is accepted that inspection is an old concept mainly denotes control and maintenance of schools. It is very rigid and authoritarian. Professional guidance to teachers does not find an important place in its ambit. The age-old system of inspection is, in brief, fault finding and coercive.

It has been rightly observed by the Study Group on Supervision and Inspection, "The old concept of 'inspection', is to some extent authoritarian and rigid, with the element of professional guidance to teachers not significantly present.... It is the inspecting officers, who 'supervise' classroom instruction because of their superior position in the administrative hierarchy. Their approach is, however, teacher-centred which does not help in the improvement of the teaching-learning process. The approach involves inspection, rating and indexing of teachers by the inspecting officers, though the method of rating in extremely subjective."

Further, the concept of inspection underwent changes and inspection was considered as service to interpret to teachers and the public the educational policies of the Government and latest educational ideas and methods. The Abbot-Wood Report has aptly remarked, "The chief duty of an inspector is to inspect schools. He must do this sympathetically and tactfully and give advice based on his own knowledge and experience which will help the teachers to make their schools enlightened and humanist institutions. He should feel free and of course be qualified to praise or to criticise; but his criticism should be calculated to encourage and not to intimidate."

(B) What is Supervision

The Dictionary of Education defines supervision as "all efforts of designated school officials towards providing leadership to teachers and other educational workers in the improvement of instruction; involves the stimulation of professional growth and development of teachers, the selection and revision of educational objectives, materials of instruction, and methods of teaching; and the evaluation of instruction." Here the word "supervision" means to guide and stimulate the activities of teachers with a view to improving them i.e., teaching as well as instruction and promoting professional growth.

Researchers and educationists agree that supervision exists for the primary purpose of improving instruction. According to Adams and Dickey, primarily "supervision is a planned programme for the improvement of instruction." It exists in their opinion, for one reason only to improve teaching and learning. Hence it is mainly concerned with "development of teachers and pupils". In short, Wiles defines supervision as assistance in the development of teaching-learning situation.

Now-a-days supervision is not concerned merely with improvement of teachers as it was conceived in the earlier days, when the supervisory activities were directive and prescriptive. It was not until the past few decades that supervision began to be seen as a cooperative and comprehensive activity. Burton and Brueckner have, therefore, visualised it as "an expert technical service primarily aimed at studying and improving cooperatively all factors which affect child growth and development. Its characteristics may be summarised as follows in outline:

1. Modern supervision directs attention towards the fundamentals of education and orients learning and its improvement within the general aim of education.
2. The aim of supervision is the improvement of the total teaching-learning process, the total setting for learning, rather than the narrow and limited aim of improving teachers in service.
3. The focus is on the selling for learning not on a person or group of persons. All persons are co-workers aiming at the improvement of a situation. One group is not superior to another, operating to "improve" the inferior group.
4. The teacher is removed from his embarrassing position as the focus of attention and the weak link in the educational process. He assumes his rightful position as a cooperating member of a group concerned with the improvement of learning.

Wiles envisages supervision as supporting, assisting and sharing rather than directing. Burton and Brueckner have gone a step ahead is this direction and have proclaimed, "Primary function of supervisors of all types is leadership, plus the encouragement and recognition of leadership in any other person either on the professional staff or among the community participants." According to some experts supervision requires a super + vision-a superior perspective attained by special preparation and position. In the complexities of the present social structure and educational process supervision has to make rational choices. As Lucio and McNeil have mentioned, "Therefore, it seems fitting to designate the supervisor as a leader who has possession of two properties: one, a clear perspective of the school's goals and awareness of its resources and qualities, and two, the ability to help others contribute to this vision and to perceive and to act in accordance with it."

Supervision centres round the basic concept of instructional improvement through leadership and cooperation of all the agencies concerned. Neagy and Evans have cogently remarked, "In summary, then, modern school supervision is positive, democratic action aimed at the improvement of classroom instruction through the continued growth of all concerned—the child, the teacher, the supervisor, the administrator and the parent or other interested lay person." Barr and Burton have thus very rightly pointed out The aim of supervision is the improvement of teaching. But this can be facilitated through the development of the teacher, the growth of the pupil and the improvement of the teaching-learning process as a whole. Consequently, supervision has to be "a cooperative effort," and "a shared relationship job."

The democratic concept of supervision thus demands constant efforts on the part of inspecting officers to stimulate, coordinate and guide the continued growth of the teacher in a school, both individually and collectively in better understanding and more effective performance of all teaching activities so that they may be better able to stimulate and guide the continued growth of every pupil towards the richest and most intelligent participation in modern democratic society. This new concept is based on the belief that inspection and supervision is a cooperative enterprise in which both the teacher and the inspecting officers have to participate actively. They should be acquainted with the problems of each other and work as a team. Brigg and Justman had streamlined the same thesis earlier, "In general supervision means to coordinate, stimulate and direct the growth of every teachers in the power to stimulate and direct the growth of every individual pupil through the exercise of his talents towards the richest and the most intelligent participation m the civilization in which he lives." On the whole, supervision through improving the teaching-learning process promotes the development of better education for youth of the society.

(C) Kinds of Supervision

In every country of the world from the earlier times to the recent days there have been a number of varieties of educational supervision, each of them reflecting certain objectives and perspectives concerning teaching-learning situations, school organisation and curriculum. An excellent statement of such kinds of supervision is made by Burton and Brueckner in the following manner, i.e., (i) inspection, (ii) laissez-faire, (iii) coercive, (iv) training and guidance, (v) democratic leadership. Elsbree and McNally have rightly opined that whereas it is not possible to draw sharp chronological lines between these five types, they seem to have developed rough in that order. It is important to note, however, that none of them is an extinct museum piece as yet; all five types are still to be found in American schools as in any other country, both eastern and western.

Inspection: Supervision, in its earlier form was merely confined to the inspection of the work of teachers and the person who was responsible for this job was popularly known as school inspector. This term is still in vogue in the supervisory services of England, India and some other countries. In United States this function was accomplished by a lay member of the school trustees or board of education. As the number of schools increased by leaps and bounds, this duty was delegated to administrative and supervisory officers. Inspection was intended to ascertain whether or not teachers were performing their normal duties and to replace the unsuitable teachers with suitable ones.

Laissez-faire: In the words of Elsbre and McNally, "the laissez-faire type of supervision is actually not constructive supervision at all. It is a policy of letting each teacher to teach as he pleases, without reference to other teacher's efforts. Little effort is made to assist teachers to improve the instructional programme or to develop any consensus among teachers with respect to philosophy or practice." This type of supervision was once dominating the domain of earlier American education. It still exists at some places. Like economic laissez-faire, it is mistaken with democracy. The officer with such type of supervision proudly remarks, "I let my teachers do as they like. No autocratic dictation to my teachers here." Their hands off policy hampers the improvement of the learning programme and reduce their status and position as professional leaders.

Coercive: It is an authoritarian concept which attributes to some authority of omniscience necessary to make momentous decisions. Nobody ever questions the validity and feasibility of such decisions. Teachers are to carry on the orders and instructions of the coercive supervisor. Such supervisors find it easy to believe that the most effective means of making teachers to work is to compel them to teach scheduled subject-matter on the stereotyped methods. Teachers are visited by them while leaching and defects or good points are made them known. They are coerced to follow the dictates of the supervisor and are awarded increments or prizes on the basis of his personal judgement.

Such type of supervision is criticized on the ground that it is based on certain erroneous assumptions. It is ridiculous to entertain the idea that some "authority" should decide things whimsically and single-handedly, which would affect the work of teachers and pupils. Any sort of coercion is detrimental to the growth of originality, ingenuity and creativeness. Such supervision does not respect the personalities of teachers and is not consistent with democracy. It violates the tenets of good mental hygiene producing the feelings of inadequacy, insecurity, frustration and fears and it is destructive of good human relationships causing teachers to conceal their weaknesses in which they are in need of help and guidance.

Though coercive supervision is not desirable, it is not always untenable. Elsbree and McNally have pointed out therefore, that those who employ it do so with the best of intentions and their ultimate objective is that of all of us to improve the quality of education. Such persons are often unaware that they are acting in an autocratic fashion and that they are working under false assumptions. Like all of us, they are educators performing their jobs in the manner they believe best. It is however to be agreed upon that such type of supervision was in vogue in other countries and is still dominating our country's educational setup.

Training and Guidance: It is now increasingly recognised that true learning should be based on understanding, interests and active participation of learners, not on rote memorization, coercion and passive listening. Education is a "process of guiding growth." Learner's voluntary cooperation in the learning process is of utmost significance. This change has brought to bear its impact on supervision. Instead of trying to compel teachers to adopt certain methods, emphasis is laid on the teaching of teachers. Supervision assumes the role of imparting in-service education and training on the job. Teachers are motivated to do better and supervision becomes a process of teaching. Consequently, the belief prevails that supervisor has the 'word' and superiority of greater knowledge and experience. As Elsbree and McNally have observed, 'It is still assumed that it is the teacher's duty to 'improve' the pattern approved by the 'superiors'. Many authorities observe that this type of instructional supervision now dominates the educational scene.

Democratic Leadership: Democracy is not merely a political organisation or procedure, it is a way of life and its principles apply to all aspects of life. Democratic ideals imply belief in common man, recognition of the dignity and worth of the individual, appreciation of the importance of individual differences as well as similarities and the assumption of authority by consent of the group. Applied to supervision, democratic ideals do not allow the imposition of the will of the supervisor upon teachers who on the other hand cannot go their own way without helping to achieve goals commonly determined. Cooperation of teachers and supervisors on the problems of improving instruction is the inherent and basic concept of democratic supervision. As Adams and Dickey have put it, "Democratic supervision builds upon the power of teacher to exercise self-direction through his participation in the determination of goals and formulation of methods and procedures for improving instruction.

The purpose of modern supervision as democratic professional leadership is subtly different from the fourth type of supervision already mentioned. According to Elsbree and McNally, instead of focussing its attention directly on the teacher, it concerns itself with the "improvement of the total teaching-iearning situation. "Today's teachers are less in need of training in service, more in need of able leadership to foster their growth as teachers and to coordinate their efforts to operate a good school. The modern supervision aims at providing leadership in improving instructional situation and in doing so, help growing professional competency. Instead of telling teachers how better to do their jobs, the supervisor works with them in the study and analysis of the total teaching-learning situations in efforts to find out how to improve that situation. In this context S. Nath has rightly developed the concept of "supervision through participation" and Burton and Brueckner have noted that "the improvement of teachers is not so much a supervisory function in which teachers participate as it is a teacher function in which supervisors cooperate. "The supervisor's function is to "release and coordinate" not to control the creative abilities of teachers.

(D) Types of Supervision and Inspection

According to some, supervision or inspection is divided into three types: (i) the corrective type, (ii) the preventive type, and (iii) the creative type.

(i) *The corrective type:* The Inspecting Officer under this type pays visits to schools with a view to finding out faults and mistakes with the methods of teaching, progress of students, maintenance of records and so on. That is why this type is called as "faultfinding" or of "police character." The inspector often goes round the school with an autocratic spirit and imposes his interests and intention in a dictatorial manner. Teachers therefore do not welcome such inspection and rather feel unhappy about it. In the end of inspection a big list of defects is prepared and given in different colours in the inspection report. Since such inspection is aimed at merely rectifying the defects with the school system, it is mainly negative and not positive in nature.

(ii) *The preventive type:* Under this type, the inspector with long experience and better insight can anticipate the school problems and help the headmaster, teachers and others of a school in solving the problems faced by them. Besides, the supervisor can prevent a number of difficulties through his foresight and professional competence. As such, preventive type of inspection helps the teaching staff as well as the community to meet situations successfully. It is, therefore, more useful and meaningful than the previous type.

(iii) *The creative type:* Creativeness is usually associated with originality, initiative, inventiveness, experimentation and democratic growth. The creative supervision naturally promotes such characteristics in the school system. It gives opportunity for the exercise of original powers, endeavours in new ways of doing things, zeal in modern practices and spirit of innovations among teachers. Thus the entire school system breathes in a free, fresh and frank atmosphere and makes teachers cooperative, resourceful and enthusiastic under this type of creative supervision. Teachers and pupils are thus encouraged to contribute their best in their performances. This type of supervision stimulates their new ideas and inspires them to make experiment with their new ideas. As such the entire school system becomes developing, democratic and creative under such supervision.

In another way, the Kothari Commission have suggested two varieties: (i) the annual inspection, and (ii) the triennial inspection. The first one will be too sketchy and another will be a thorough inspection. The annual inspection should be just a departmental affair and be carried out by the officers of the proposed District School Boards for the Primary Schools and by the officers of the State Education Departments for the Secondary Schools. The triennial inspection will be organised by a panel consisting of an inspecting officer, two or three headmasters or teachers of primary or secondary schools as the case may be.

(E) Nature and Characteristics of Modern Supervision

"Modern supervision at its finest" said Neagley and Evans, is both dynamic and democratic reflecting the vitality of enlightened and informed leadership. All human beings in the educative process—students, teachers, administrators and supervisors—are individuals of worth, endowed with unique talents and capacities. The primary aim of supervision must be to recognize the inherent value of each person, to the end that the full potential of all will be realized. "The philosophy of democracy, the psychology of group dynamics, inter-personal relationships, professional leadership etc. have left indelible imprint on the theory and practice of modern supervision. In the democratic social order, education is a dynamic force. Hence supervision becomes dynamic in character.

1. Modern 'Supervision is Democratic and Cooperative in Spirit and Organization

Democracy does not mean "laissez-faire", which let everybody go one's own way. Rather it implies a dynamic, understanding and cooperative leadership role. Supervision is concerned with providing effective leadership and implies cooperative working relationships. Jennings has depicted leaders as those persons who have greater emotional maturity than the members of the group and have greater insight into the needs of the persons with whom they work. Modern supervision is based on the assumption that education is a creative and cooperative enterprise, in which all teachers, pupils, parents and administrators participate and supervisors are their academic leaders who stimulate, guide and advise them in improvement of instruction. Lewin, comparing authoritarian with democratic leadership observes that in a group with democratic leadership there are more objective attitudes, more cooperative effort, more constructive suggestion, greater feelings of "we-ness" and more feeling of joint goals. Modern supervision must foster all these qualities.

2. Modern Supervision is Established on Maintenance of Satisfactory Inter-personal Relationship

Supervision succeeds only to the extent that each person involved is regarded as a human being with a unique contribution to make in the educative process. Neagley and Evans have visualised that relationship of supervisors among all personnel must be friendly, open, informal, and congenial. Better human relationships are demanded by the present world. It is imperative that supervision must develop and maintain a high level of personal interaction. Otherwise it would be ineffective and unproductive. According to Wiles, "A group's productiveness is affected by the quality of its human relations, and the supervisor must work constantly for the improvement of group cohesiveness." The supervisor cannot but be concerned with improving group feeling, group morale, and group unity.

3. Modem Supervision Must be Communicative

The supervisor is concerned with communication within a group as leadership depends on better social interaction. Researches have revealed that good communication is related to good morale of teachers and free exchange of information helps in good planning. To improve communication, the supervisor should increase his skill as a discussion leader, to provide the physical facilities that facilitate communication and to improve the group processes. As Wiles has observed, "If a supervisor hopes to facilitate communication, he will work for decrease in status lines, for constant study of the processes used in the group, and for desirable physical structure and competent group leadership."

4. Modern Supervision is Comprehensive in Scope

It embraces the total school programmes and proper articulation is necessary through all the supervisory agencies. Unlike the earlier supervision, the modern type is wider in scope not merely focussing on criticism of the teacher in the classroom. Neagley and Evans have rightly said, "Today, supervision is directed at improving all factors involved in pupil learning. Gone are the days of attempting to improve the teacher without regard to the totality of the teaching-learning situation in the school. The modern supervisor's role reaches far beyond the traditional classroom visitation."

5. Modem Supervision is Creative

Teaching is an art; supervision is a creative work. The purpose of supervision is to draw out the best in teachers to ignite their latent talents, to stimulate the initiative, to encourage their originality and self-expression. It emphasizes their success and strengths and makes their weakness and failures side issues. The supervisor should have new ideas, resourcefulness and original thinking. The modern supervisor should know how to present facts in a pleasant way and to work resourcefully.

6. Modern Supervision is Scientific

The supervisor makes use of scientific methods to effect improvement in instruction. Through surveys, experiments, action researches he should make his performances more scientific and effective. He will encourage constructive and critical thinking among teachers and discourage flattering and biased opinions.

7. Modern Supervision is Experimental and Auto-Critical in Nature

In contrast to autocratic and authoritarian type, the emerging concept of supervision stimulates experimentalism and self-criticism. Neagley and Evans have amply explained that one of the foundation stones of the emerging philosophy and practice of supervision is the belief that current practice should always be questioned and evaluated and placed under the searching light of critical analysis. Any aspect of the learning situation found to be ineffective or detrimental to the achievement of better situation, is dropped or modified accordingly. The supervisor leads his teachers in the constant search for better and more effective ways of doing their job, believing always that no best way is ever been found.

(F) Agencies of Modern Supervision

The emerging theory of supervision is so comprehensive, broad, flexible and dynamic that it embraces a large number of services and personnel within its ambit. In the United States the number and kind of personnel involved in supervisory services have been varied and multifarious. During the early eighteenth century, certain lay men from the trustees were being appointed as inspectors. Now there has been a steady expansion to include members of state departments of education, superintendents, supervisors, special supervisors, directors, coordinators, departmental heads and resource personnel or helping teachers. Wiles has made this point amply clear by asserting: "Supervision is not limited to any one person or to individuals, who carry the title 'supervisor'. Any member of the school staff may assist teachers in providing a better learning environment for pupils. In fact, probably most supervision is provided by teachers for other teachers."

In this line, Adams and Dickey have eloquently explained the practices and persons involved in supervisory services prevalent in United States. They have stated that a supervisor may be the principal of a school in a small system, the building principal in a large system, a supervisor of a special field such as physical education, art or music, the director or elementary education, a director of instruction in a country or city school system, the country or city school superintendent, or a helping teacher. All these persons may deal with problems specifically related to the improvement of the instructional programme; they may have primary duty for improving conditions of learning situation and for helping each others to be more effective in guiding the learning experiences of pupils. The degree to which these supervisory services accomplish the duties mentioned is the real measure of their distinction and effectiveness,

With this measuring rod in our hand, we may in our conditions include head teachers, assistant teachers, coordinators, inspecting officers and even Block Development Officers and Chairman, Panchayat Samities under supervisory services (for primary schools). Because all these personnel contribute to instruction and facilitate the improvement of teaching-learning situation in our schools. Wiles has cogently stated, "Supervision has been recognised as a process and not identified with a position. With this change in concept, the role of the person labelled as supervisor has changed. He is concerned with facilitating the process of supervision. Hence a supervisor is not a person, who merely supervises, but expedites the process of supervision for improving instruction of pupils. As such, agencies of supervision are ranging from top to bottom and are multi-situational.

(G) Meaning of Administration and its Difference from Supervision

Adam and Dickey have rightly said that to separate supervision and administration on the basis of function alone is a virtual impossibility. Some overlapping of supervisory and administrative functions is inevitable. As we know supervisory service is particularly concerned with instruction and its improvement. It is directly concerned with teaching and learning and with the factors included in and related to these processes—the teacher, the pupil, the curriculum, the instructional materials etc. On the other hand, administration is aimed at the same goals as supervision, but not directly. Budget-making, construction of building, personnel administration, and so on are all intended to improve the educational programmes. Though all these activities result in more effective learning of the pupil, it is achieved not immediately or directly. In other words, administrative functions are concerned with material facilities, whereas supervisory services are concerned with improving the learning or academic situation.

Administration must see that continuous improvement of the instructional programme by supervisory services is accomplished. Administration, therefore, creates an organization for supervision, employ, assign, direct and supervise the supervisors. He has aptly said, "All of this means that supervision is an arm of administration and that the total organisation for supervision must be an integral part of the administrative organisation for the school system as a whole." Similarly many administrative problems cannot be solved wisely without the care of instruction which is the primary concern of supervision. Administration is responsible for providing school buildings, books, instructional supplies, selection and appointment of teachers etc. But what kind of teachers for what kind of an instructional programme? What type and size of classrooms with what kind of physical facilities for what kind of instructional programme? Hence there must be cordial and intimate working relationships between administration and supervision.

Though administration and supervision are related in so many important ways, it is not difficult to differentiate the process of supervision from the process of administration. The latter in its roles of policy formation, decision-making, direction and control, may not always have the teaching learning elements. Sears in distinguishing between administration and supervision makes it crystal clear that supervision is mainly an academic or teaching function. Modern supervision has its essential functions of promoting and guiding teaching-learning situations. The dynamics of supervision should be consistent with good teaching process i.e. growth and development of the learner. On the whole supervisory services essentially and basically are aimed at promoting and facilitating improvement of instruction, which is the goal of elementary school programme. In spite of overlapping of administrative and supervisory services, Neagley and Evans have rightly said that any leadership function which is primarily concerned with the improvement of class-room instruction or curriculum development will be considered supervisory.

In India it is usually found that the administrative work-load of inspecting officers is so heavy that their legitimate function of supervision for improvement of the teaching-learning process is seriously neglected. The separation of administration from supervision is therefore strongly advised by a number of experts and bodies. This step is expected to enable the supervisors to devote more time and energy to the improvement of education, particularly the teaching-learning process. According to one of the Directive Principles of the Constitution, separation between the judiciary and the executive has already been brought about. Analogically separation of administrative responsibilities from supervisory duties should be made as soon as possible. In this context, the Study Group on Supervision and Inspection have rightly spelt out the following reasons for such separation.

(a) The educational administrator derives and fashions his image from the general administrator in other departments like Revenue, Law and Order etc.

(b) The exercise of administrative power is more prestigious and is also a status symbol.

(c) Lapses in administration catch the immediate attention of the public, the Parliament (State Legislature) and the higher authorities of the Government.

(d) Academic functions presuppose certain scholarly attitudes and habits of study which are harder to attain.

It may not be out of place to refer to the recommendations made by the Kothari Commission on this issue. The Commission has suggested that District School Boards should be set up and one of their functions should be to look after management and administration, leaving the District Educational Officer (Circle/District Inspector of Schools) and his staff to concentrate on supervision and inspection. While the Commission emphasized the importance of these two wings working in close collaboration, it was, however, of the view that when differences arise, the last word should be either with the District Educational Officer or Director of Education (Director of Public Instruction). Such an arrangement, in the opinion of the Commission, would enable the inspecting officers to concentrate on supervision i.e. on the improvement of instruction, guidance to teachers, organisation of in-service education, provision of extension services.

2

Role, Functions and Techniques of Supervision

(A) The Role of Supervision

Modern societies are making fantastic yet exciting demands upon the schools. The continuing explosion of man's knowledge staggers imagination and leads to increasing intellectual and vocational specialization in any highly complex society. It is humanly impossible for one to master any significant amount of this accumulated knowledge of mankind. But man being a total being an entity, Neagley and Evans have observed, "He must be able to coordinate his various experiences into a meaningful whole if he is to lead a productive life and be reasonably adjusted physically, mentally, socially and emotionally."

Since modern school curriculum represents ideally the sum and substance of man's most important experiences, ideals, values, attitudes and aspirations, there is pressing need in every school system to decide what to teach and how to teach. The astounding increase in the quantum of knowledge is accompanied with multifarious number and varieties of instructional media such as programmed learning materials, instructional films, and educational television. There are also new experiments in organizational patterns as team teaching, upgraded units and the like. All such changes naturally result in increasing rate of obsolescence in content, methods, media and practices. In the developing countries like India, therefore, many other problems both academic and administrative like wastage, stagnation, mass or universal education, falling standards, national integration, which are extremely challenging and complicating.

Under these circumstances, supervisory services are destined to play an important role in deciding the nature and content of curriculum, in selecting the school organization patterns and learning materials to facilitate teaching in giving guidance for professional growth of teachers and making new experiments, researches etc. and in evaluating the entire educational process. Effective coordination and leadership are essentially required by supervisory services.

Venkat Swamy has rightly pointed out that need for effective supervision is felt more in India than in any other advanced countries in the world. In the advanced countries like U.S.A. and U.K. teachers are highly qualified both academically and professionally. They have enough of educational literature to improve their professional efficiency. There are strong teachers' organisations like NEA and NUT which are financially sound to run the orientation courses and undertaking research and experiments for the benefit of teachers. Supervisors have, therefore, practically a less important role to play in the qualitative improvement of education in those countries. But in India the conditions are quite different. Almost all the school teachers in rural area are not adequately qualified. They have neither sufficient educational literature, nor much facilities for in-service education to improve their proficiency. Hence the role of supervisory services is more significant in India for imparting effective education than in most of the developed countries.

(B) Function and Scope of Supervision

Supervisory functions may mainly be divided into two categories: (i) Administrative and (ii) Academic of course, real supervision should not have any administrative responsibilities. But as has been discussed earlier, there are not any clear-cut barriers between administration and supervision and both go hand in hand, in actual situations, the supervisor has also to discharge a large number of administrative tasks. Especially under Indian conditions the inspecting officers have to perform many administrative functions. These administrative duties may briefly be mentioned as follows:

1. Selection and appointment of subordinate teaching and menial staff.
2. Sanction and payment of grants and remuneration.
3. Providing physical facilities to schools and subordinate officers.
4. Recognition and gradation of schools.
5. Holding of scholarship examinations and awarding scholarships.
6. Approving resolutions of the managing committees and seeing the managing committees function properly.
7. Checking the accounts and records of schools.
8. Checking the safety and security of the school plant.
9. Maintaining proper service-conditions and eliminating grievances of teachers in time.
10. Checking proper distribution of work-load.

The academic functions of the supervisor are multifarious. But some of them may be stated as below:

1. Supervision of instruction.
2. Maintenance of standards.
3. Guidance and demonstration of lessons and experiments.
4. Orientation of teachers through in-service training courses, seminars, staff-meetings, conferences etc.
5. Evaluation and assessment of pupils' achievement.
6. Verifying the proper maintenance of school records, like cumulative records, examination registers, progress cards etc.
7. Preparation of instructional materials like handbooks, guide-books, lesson notes, scheme of lessons etc.
8. Supervising the organisation of co-curricular activities.
9. Conducting surveys, researches and experimentation.
10. Coordinating the activities of the Board of Secondary Education, State Institute of Education with those of schools follow-up and feed-back activities.

The important duties and functions of the supervisor may be spelt out as follows:

1. Supervision of Curricular Instruction

The supervisor is mainly responsible for academic or curricular activities of the school. He therefore, supervises the actual class-teaching, methods followed, and audio-visual aids used to make teaching interesting and effective. Thus he evaluates the efficiency of teachers as well as the progress and standards of students in schools. In this context he has to verify the time-table scheme of lessons and lesson plans of the school in order to know how far the work-load has been equitably distributed among the teachers, how far the prescribed course of studies has been covered in different classes and how various topics are dealt in the classes.

2. Supervision of Co-curricular Activities

Modern education does not mean merely the teaching of three R's. It is much broader than this. Students have to be provided with various co-curricular activities like games and sports, debates, student-government, school magazine, school museum, drama, school exhibition and the like, which promote different talents and aptitudes of individual students. These activities are nevertheless essential for growth of democratic habits and training for citizenship. Hence the supervisor is expected to supervise the co-curricular activities and see that they are properly organised and made successful.

3. Supervision of School Plant

The supervisor is also concerned with adequacy, safety and security of the school plant, as the physical facilities are the means of organising both curricular and co-curricular programmes and practices. Besides, he is also required to see that proper discipline, healthy habits and general conduct of students as well as the staff-members are maintained and promoted. He should also supervise the cleanliness of the school campus, beautification of the school buildings and surroundings, suitable drinking water facilities, security of electrical fittings, neatness of urinals and latrines. He should check up such arrangements and amenities and advise the concerned authorities on their safety, security and adequacy for the welfare of students and staff.

4. Supervision of the School Office

School office is called the nerve-centre of the school. Different records, registers, reports and preformed are preserved there; important administrative and academic matters are discussed there and the head master does almost all his desk-work there. Proper maintenance of the records and safely of the registers and discipline of the school office depend on the efficiency of the headmaster. Unless the office is safeguarded, management of the school will be in jeopardy. The supervisor should, therefore, look into it and check up the up-to-date and proper maintenance of records and registers, especially those dealing with financial matters and permanent data.

5. Supervision of Developmental Programmes

The supervisor is not only responsible for the adequate use and maintenance of the school plant including accommodation, furniture and apparatus, but also he has to see its developmental aspects. In this connection he has to see the prospects of its expansion- extension of buildings, increase of enrolment, provision of more equipments and furniture, opening of new sections, classes, introduction of new subjects and soon. He should examine the various arrangements and practices with a view to serving the local community. The participation and association of school staff and students in the cultural and recreational programmes of the society should also be verified and advised upon by the supervisor.

(C) Techniques of Supervision

The supervisor has to adopt a number of techniques for making his supervision effective and successful. These techniques may broadly be divided into two categories: (i) Group techniques, and (ii) Individual techniques.

(i) Group Techniques

(1) Curriculum construction and development should be done cooperatively by the teachers and supervisors with a view to making learning experiences of the students worthwhile and up-to-date. This will promote improved courses of study, better staff understanding and relationships, improved articulation among the various school units such as primary and secondary schools and a general awakening of interest in new trends of methodology and school organisation.

(2) Continuous in-service, education should be provided by the supervisor in a carefully planned manner on the basis of felt needs and requirements of the teachers. This will enable teachers to get up-to-date knowledge in content, methods of teaching and school organisation.

(3) Research and experimentation should be undertaken in collaboration with the teachers. Especially action research is extremely needed in our educational system not only to make our teachers problem-conscious, but also to help their problem-solving capacities, which, in the long run, develop their professional competence as well as the teaching-learning process.

(4) Adequate orientation of teachers to the school and community is an important supervisory function. The better school-community relations besides facilitating the solution of many day-to-day problems, help in organising curricular and co-curricular programmes.

(5) Co-ordination of good practices and innovations is an essential function of the supervisor. Isolation prevailing among various schools can be broken and tried out good practices existing in one school should be published and propagated among others for encouraging the innovator and for reaping the good fruits of such innovations.

(6) The supervisor has to deliver demonstration lessons himself and arrange such lessons by experienced and skilful teachers and experts. The centre-meetings should be energised where

not only demonstration or model lessons and experiments will be conducted, but also discussions on them and other relevant matters can be made effectively.

(7) Exhibitions of books, illustrative and instructional materials should be arranged by supervisors on various occasions. Training for preparation of audio-visual aids should be organised by supervisors.

(8) Inter-school visits, study tours, and educational trips can be organised for teachers with a view to giving them opportunities to gain new insight and valuable experiences for improving educational programmes and practices.

(9) Educational conferences, seminars and study groups may be organised, where teachers, experts and supervisors cooperatively discuss various problems confronting them and find solutions.

(10) It is felt useful to issue circulars and publish bulletins for dismantling new ideas and information as regards some modern trends, practices and innovations among teachers.

(11) Staff-meeting is a vital part of supervision. Without this supervision should not be complete. The supervisor discusses different problems and issues felt in course of his inspection of a particular school. The headmaster and teachers may seek certain clarification and advice on the occasion from the supervisor. They are naturally benefited by the superior knowledge, skill and expertise of the supervisor through such discussion. Thus the supervisor helps solving the problems of the school and extend necessary guidance to teachers.

These and such other group techniques are essential for making supervision effective and operative. Especially under our situations where the number of schools and teachers is enormous and supervisors are not able to inspect schools at least once in a year, techniques of group dynamics are more feasible and successful. Moreover, school complexes, centre-meetings etc. should be well-organised with a view to utilising group techniques.

(ii) Individual Techniques

(1) Visiting classroom-teaching is an important techniques of supervision. The supervisor will not be able to understand the curriculum in action unless the supervisor visit classes regularly. If satisfactory human relations exist, supervisors will feel free to supervise classes and teachers will welcome them. The purpose of this technique will not fault-finding, but sensing the real working of the curriculum, feeling the adequacy of the pupils' learning experiences and ascertaining the teachers' competencies. On the basis of these experiences, supervisor has to plan and organise in-service training programmes as well as school curriculum.

(2) The supervisor has to create occasions for meeting the individual teachers and for giving advice on different matters. Neagley and Evans (p. 8) have said, "Individual teacher conferences should be prominent in any comprehensive supervisory plan. These are usually held after classroom visitations or at the request of the teacher or supervisor. They can be most valuable in providing for an exchange of ideas; in giving an opportunity for constructive suggestions about classroom techniques or materials of instruction; and in identifying possible areas for curriculum study or for professional growth of the teacher."

(3) One of the functions of supervision is to take professional leadership. But to explore and encourage leadership among competent teachers is an important technique of democratic supervision. The supervisor cannot make himself available to all teachers requiring academic advice and enlightenment. But if adequate number of teachers are advanced professionally, they will be able to discharge some supervisory functions. Many teaching-learning problems can be avoided or solved through the growth of such local professional leadership among teachers.

(4) The encouragement of professional writing by teachers is a technique of the supervision. Through this, efficient teachers with proper literary aptitude, will be able to contribute to the

enrichment of professional literature and help increasing competence of teachers.

(5) Similarly research and experimentation in new methods of teaching and school organisation should be undertaken by talented and resourceful teachers. But in' this direction the supervisor has to provide suitable incentive and academic guidance.

3

Objectives, Principles, Organisation and Planning of Supervision

(A) Objectives and Principles of Supervision

There is a saying, "The star is useful, though the mariner never reaches." Ideals are always desirable. Objectives are always necessary. The formulation of objectives is of utmost importance for effective supervision as it is geared and orientated towards the particular objectives. Otherwise it is apt to lose its aims and is likely to be misled and misdirected. The aims and objectives are like the compass in the ship. The curriculum planning, organisation of learning experiences, use of audio-visual aids, methods of teaching and even the system of school organisation are shaped and influenced by the aims and objectives of supervision. If the supervisor is autocratic, freedom and democratic spirit among teachers will not be available.

Objectives are mainly of two kinds: (i) general, and (ii) specific. If improvement of the teaching-learning process is taken as general objective of supervision, interpreting the school programmes to the community may be regarded as one of the specific objectives of supervision. On the other hand, from the point of view of time-factor, objectives can be classified into two: (i) long-term, and (ii) short-term. The objectives which are formulated to be realised through a long time are long-term objectives, and which are to be achieved within a short period are short-term objectives. For instance, evaluating teachers' performance in terms of pupils' growth and educational objectives may be taken as a long-term objective, and to organise an in-service training course for making up content-deficiency of a group of primary school teachers may be regarded as a short-term objective.

Some of the important objectives of supervision are as follows:

(1) Traditionally or as it is well known to all concerned, main objective of supervision is the evolution of the school programme. That is, the supervisor is expected to assess the growth of the child and the effectiveness of the teaching-learning process.

(2) To provide professional leadership to all educational workers under his jurisdiction is an important objective of the supervisor. Such leadership is felt essential to improve the teachers' competence and guide them on the right direction.

(3) Identifying the various factors responsible for promoting or hindering the teaching-learning process and taking necessary steps to utilise or control these forces is a useful task for the supervisor.

(4) To ascertain the strengths and weaknesses of the schools and to set suitable goals or targets for progress of the educational institutions is the objective of supervision.

(5) Participation and involvement of the supervisor in the actual teaching-learning process and to help solving the educational problems faced by the teachers as well as pupils is a function of the supervisor.

(6) Sharing with the public the school problems and getting support for their solutions is an objective of supervision.

(7) Assisting teachers to identify and analyse learning difficulties and other educational problems of pupils and helping them in planning suitable remedial instruction is a function of the supervisor.

(8) Evaluating teachers' performance in terms of pupils' growth and educational objectives and suggest ways and means in the direction is an aim of supervision.

(9) Assisting and encouraging the teachers' preparation of instructional materials like handbooks, guidebooks, workbooks, scheme of lessons, lesson-plans and the like is an objective of supervision.

(10) Promoting professional growth of all teachers through provision of in-service education like training courses, staff discussion, writing and reading educational materials and so no.

(11) Undertaking research and experiment himself and with participation of teachers is an objective of supervision. This will give him new insight into the different educational problems and help solving them. In brief, supervision is intended to improve the quality of instruction by promoting the professional growth of all teachers. Barr and Burton have very cogently said, "The aim of supervision is the improvement of teaching" and Douglass, Bent and Boardman have rightly remarked, "The whole purpose of supervision is the development of better education for youth."

(B) Organization of Supervision

Every organisation is a social unit or a human group constructed and reconstructed for achieving certain specific objectives. Organization of supervision is, therefore, the system of supervisory personnel which is structured and restructured in course of time to realize the aims and objectives of supervision. Therefore, many kinds of organizations have been evolved and in vogue in different countries at different times. Some of the important varieties are discussed below:

(1) *Line and Staff Variety:* Line organization is primarily involved in a direct flow of authority upward and downward. A line officer has power and authority over the subordinates. He is a generalist who discharges mainly administrative functions. The examples of such line officers are Director of Public Instruction, District Inspector of Schools or Deputy Inspector of Schools. In this system, delegation of powers is made by the superior officers to subordinate officers.

On the other hand, staff officers do not stand in the direct line of descending or ascending authority. They, of course, sometimes exercise line authority and may be divided into three types according to the functions they perform: (i) service, (ii) coordinative and (iii) advisory. The instances of staff personnel are officers for NCC, Evaluation, Educational Technology, Hindi and so on. The staff officers generally render technical service, guidance and advice to the department and as such are usually specialised.

Although the line and staff patterns of supervision and administration are considerably criticised, there is no way of abolishing either line or staff personnel without impairing efficiency and expediency. It is, therefore, suggested that such patterns have to be mended rather than ended. The important point is that these services should be organised democratically. Delegation of authority, involvement of subordinate officers in planning and their sharing in decision-making should be made to the maximum and number of authority levels and line officers be kept at a minimum. Thus in the present set up both line and staff personnel are reconciled and made use of for better supervision and administration. Coordination between them is, however, essential for efficiency. The structure will be as follows:

Head of Department

(Director)

Line Officers	Staff Officers
(Deputy Director.,	(N. C. C Guidance,
C.I., D.I. of Schools,	Physical Education,
Principal etc.)	Science Education etc.)

(2) *Administrative and Academic Type:* As discussed earlier, organization of supervision has long since been composite and dualistic in nature having both administrative and academic features and functions. Although attempts have been made to separate one from the other in order to eradicate injustice and malpractice as well as to increase efficiency in the organization, complete bifurcation has not yet been possible. The inspecting officers at all levels perform functions of both administration and supervision. Since they devote much of their time and energy to administrative functions, their main supervisory duties are considerably neglected. Therefore, various educational committees and commissions have suggested that separation of administration from supervision is necessary for the betterment of education. The States of Maharashtra and Andhra

Pradesh have already introduced reforms in the field of educational supervision by entrusting administration and management of schools to the Zilla Parishads with a number of officials and by keeping the inspecting officers entirely free for intensive supervision. The structure of organization will be as follows:

Directorate of Education

Administrative Wing	Academic Wing
(Zilla Parishad, Panchayat Samities and others)	(Supervisory Personnel with S.I.E.)

In some other States like Orissa, Administrative officers are appointed in the Directorates in order to assist the Directors in performing the administrative functions, so that more time and energy can be spared for supervisory work. Similarly, Deputy Inspectors are being attached to the Inspectorate for the same purpose. But it is a doubt whether such arrangement is improving supervision to cover expectation.

(3) *Vertical and Horizontal Type*: When a particular officer is required *to* supervise certain aspects is all the stages of education beginning from the lowest to the highest rung of the educational ladder, that kind of organization is called the vertical type. If an officer invariably an expert in Mathematics will visit all kinds of institutions both lower and higher and give advice and guidance to the concerned teachers for improvement of the teaching of the subject, then it will be an example of the vertical type of supervision. But in the horizontal type of organization a class of personnel are required to supervise only a particular stage of education. They are naturally expected to see all the subjects at a stage. For example, a Sub-Inspector of Schools supervises all subjects taught in all kinds of primary schools and a Circle Inspector of Schools has to supervise all subjects taught in all kinds of secondary schools. Thus the horizontal type of organization has a very close resemblance to our present type of supervision. As a result, coordination in the teaching of various subjects is possible in the horizontal system of supervision, whereas in vertical system such coordination at a particular stage will be absent. Similarly, coordination in the teaching of a particular subject at various stages

is feasible under the vertical system of supervision, whereas it will be a difficult task under the horizontal organization of supervision.

At present, attempts are made to wave a coordinated type of supervision for effective teaching-learning activities. Under this system both vertical and horizontal kinds of organization are made use of. For example, a body of experts from all teaching subjects will be appointed to bring about coordination among all subjects at various stages. In U.S.A. such practice is in vogue. The Kothari Commission have also suggested the "panel supervision" or "team teaching" for effecting desirable coordination in teaching as well as in supervision.

Obviously, no single pattern of organization for supervision will satisfactorily serve all our purposes for all time to come. In response to changing conditions in the educational objectives, school organization and administrative set up, there must be corresponding reforms in the organization and programmes of supervision.

(C) Planning of Supervision

Planning is essential for economy and efficiency in any organisation. Even an individual has to do some sort of planning either mental or written for utilising his resources including money and time in the best possible use. Otherwise there will be wastage of resources and frustration of basic objectives either of an individual or an organisation. It is now realized that there will be no good education without proper planning. With a view to making our teaching effective we draw a lesson plan; for making best use of the available resources of an institution we chalk out an institutional plan; and in order to make supervision meaningful and useful, systematic planning for it, is necessary.

As in other kinds of planning, in educational planning also there are mainly three important steps. Firstly the knowledge of needs and requirements or identification of problems is the primary stage. Without knowing the problems and needs properly and adequately, no planning for attacking these problems and fulfilling the needs will be possible. Further it will not be feasible to do them all at a time. Priorities among them have to be fixed according to urgency and necessity. Similarly, there are many administrative and academic problems to be tackled by the inspecting officer. He has to recognize or identify these problems on the basis of his experiences gained and data collected. For examples, there may be a number of schools left unvisited for a long time and should be visited soon, there may be deficiencies in the content knowledge of teachers in some subjects like English, Science etc., for which certain in-service training courses have to be organised, and such other needs to be provided for. The supervisor has to decide which schools have to be inspected earlier and in what subjects training courses have to be conducted. For these, the supervisor has to fix priorities in view of their urgency and need.

Secondly, survey of the resources available or likely to be available is important for solving the existing problems. This involves an array of human, physical and academic elements. Among human elements are teachers, pupils, parents and other employees. On the physical side, are building, equipment, funds, play grounds and the like. Besides these two, there are academic matters like curriculum, courses of study, methods of teaching, rules and regulations etc., which are also equally significant from the point of view of planning for solving the problems. The limitations, strengths and weaknesses of these resources have to be taken into consideration. The supervisor accordingly takes a stock of all the resources like funds, equipments accommodation, resource personnel etc. Before planning for in-service training courses and for paying visits to various schools scattered throughout his jurisdiction.

Thirdly, formulation of working principles or finding ways and means for solving the problems is the next step in planning. The methods and techniques for solving the academic as well as administrative problems have to be ascertained and strategies for attacking various complications have to be determined. The supervisor thus has to plan how and when different courses and programmes should be organised and implemented with which teachers and with what materials and resource personnel

Planning, besides being collective, has also to be individualized and diversified in view of the intrinsic worth, strength and weakness of different institutions. Common planning for all the educational institutions is defective. That is why, institutional planning has been suggested by various educationists and commissions as already discussed in a separate chapter. We should not expect that all the teachers and all the schools must move forward in unison. The success of educational supervision will depend upon the flexible approach where the institutions will go ahead according to their own individual pace determined by their special strengths and weaknesses. The supervisor should not take the easy line of imposing common restrictions on all or be daring enough to give equal freedom to all. The Kothari Commission have rightly suggested that the supervisor should analyse the strengths and weaknesses of each school and of each school teacher and help them make the best progress they can. One of the essential conditions for making an educational system classic and dynamic, therefore, is to develop this competence, to discriminate between school and school, between teacher and teacher and to adopt a flexible mode of planning for individuals or institutions at different levels of development. This alone can help to promote initiative, creativity and experimentation on the part of the supervisors and teachers.

4

Evaluation of Supervision and Inspection

(A) Evaluation

Evaluation is the last but not the least important phase of supervision and inspection. The end of supervision is the improvement of the teaching-learning process or making the entire educational programme successful and effective. But it is to be ascertained how far such objective has been achieved through various supervisory services and programmes. The supervisory techniques and methods have to be modified and improved upon on the basis of the assessment. The ways and means for measuring the success of supervision are however not developed so far adequately. Neagely and Evans have aptly observed, "The evaluation of supervision is somewhat like the weather; everyone talks about it, but hardly anyone has really done anything about it. Research is lacking on the means for assessing the effectiveness of a comprehensive supervisory programme".

Evaluation of supervision needs a total or comprehensive approach. The whole school programme or the entire teaching learning process has to be evaluated with a view to appraising the effectiveness of supervision. Since such evaluation naturally involves inter-human relationships and personalities to a great extent, subjective assessment plays an important role. It is, therefore, felt difficult to evaluate and ascertain fairly the contributions of teachers, supervisors and administrators. Attempts are however made and evaluative procedures are developed for scientific and objective assessment of supervision.

Primarily two approaches are suggested by Neagley and Evans (p. 278) for the comprehensive evaluation of the supervisory programmes. Firstly, the various elements of the total instructional programme must be appraised, including pupil progress towards the goals of instruction and the effectiveness of various supervisory techniques. Secondly, plans need to be developed for the evaluation of supervisory personnel, considering the role that each person is excepted to play in the improvement of instruction.

(i) *Evolution of the total programme*: Different aspects of the instructional programme should be taken into consideration and many kinds of searching questions be asked in the staff meetings and conferences. The kinds of problems faced, probable solutions, persons responsible, success and failures of various programmes and so on may be raised and discussed on such occasions. Through continuous probing, burning problems can be attacked successfully and weak or strong areas in the instructional programmes can be identified properly. Evaluation check-lists and schedules on such crucial points may be prepared cooperatively by teachers, supervisors and administrators. Pupils' progress and achievement can be evaluated by the best instruments available against the objectives of the curriculum. Questions on joint curriculum planning, use of standardized tests in intelligence, achievement and aptitude and identification of their limitations, discussion on these points, use and efficacy of different methods and materials should be discussed in this context. Thus evaluation of the various techniques used to improve instruction will help to ascertain the effectiveness of supervisory practices and techniques employed. Evaluation by outside agencies should be welcomed by all schools. Some good criteria have been developed by various academic bodies. These criteria can be used by supervisors as means of self-evaluation. Then a team of teachers, supervisors and teachers can be engaged for a detailed assessment. This will help a better understanding of the strengths and weaknesses of the current instructional programme.

Moorer (p. 150) has developed an instrument which will be valuable for self-analysis of the supervisory programme. According to him a good supervisor constantly seek to narrow the gap between what is and what might be in the supervisory programme. This implies that the supervisor has to take stock of what is and look at the present programme in the light of what might be. It is essential to know where the programme stands along the line of development from an inferior programme to a superior one. Progress along this line is possible only when thinking has gone ahead of action or realization. If the supervisor dreams for a better programme, in course of time he will explore ways and means for bringing it about and for carrying it closer to the realization of his dreams. The dreams are by nature vague and nebulous to some extent, but Moorer's instrument is designed in such a manner that its use will give substance to them with respect to what might be.

It is useful to identify some of the more important elements of an *inferior programme* and a *superior programme* of supervision. The supervisor can approximate the status of the present programme on a scale. In most instances it is likely that the programme of supervision in a circle will fall somewhere between the two extreme points on this scale. That is the problem for the supervisor to decide. Here is the scale:

1	2	3	4	5
Inferior programme	Moving toward	Average programme	Moving toward	Superior programme

Moorer says that the marking of the scale is simple. If you circle the number four (4) for *Materials and Resources,* for example, this means that in your best judgement the supervisory programme in your circle is above average and moving towards a superior programme. You also should not expect to achieve the finest possible supervisory programme by next year. But the school children and their parents have a right to except some improvement. This instrument is designed to challenge the alert supervisor. If a programme for the improvement of instruction can be worked out in terms of commonly accepted, long-range goals and the agencies and methods of realizing these goals are mutually decided, Moorer says, "things are bound to happen".

(ii) *Evaluation of the Supervisory Personnel:* The second method of evolution of supervision is the complete assessment of the work of each supervisor, both by himself and by other professional personnel.

Self-evaluation is the real key to effective analysis of one's contribution to the improvement of instruction. Some criteria and check-lists are developed for the self-appraisal of the supervisors. Wiles (pp. 291-4) outlined a number of self-evaluation procedures for supervisors. The following list of questions is suggested by him as a means of examining the way he works:

1. Do I set up a schedule of activities for each week, for each day?
2. Am I flexible in my schedule without becoming disturbed?
3. Do I get upset when my plans do not go as I hoped?
4. Do I check off the things I have accomplished?
5. Do my feelings get hurt?
6. Am I able to take criticism?
7. Am I able to put myself in the other person's position?
8. Am I making sincere effort to learn more about the staff?
9. Do I consult those who will be affected by an action before I take it?
10. Do I live up to commitments?

Wiles has further pointed that the measure of a supervisor's success lies in the worthwhile change he is able to effect and these are important questions in judging the effectiveness of a supervisor. Such check lists can be developed for each position according to the job descriptions and the working relationships and responsibilities. This suggestion should assume that line and staff functions defined according to the modern democratic principles of supervision as described earlier.

Evaluation by others: Since self-evaluation usually needs a higher standard of honesty, integrity and objectivity which is not present in many personnel, such evaluation, therefore, becomes deceptive and misleading. In order to minimise subjectivity and wrong data, it is fell essential to take the help of others in evaluation. The Educational

Research Service (p. 1) reported procedures for evaluating administrative personnel in sixty-two of the largest school districts throughout the U.S.A. From a check list on the survey instrument, the main purposes of such evaluation were indicated as follows:

1. To identify areas in which improvement is needed.
2. To assess evaluator's present performance in accordance with prescribed standards.
3. To help evaluator to establish relevant performance objectively and work systematically towards their achievement.

In the majority of the sixty-two districts, each administrator is evaluated annually by his superior. The procedures used to evaluate administrative and supervisory personnel vary in different districts and tend to fall into two categories: (i) Procedure that stress rating relating to *job-standards*, and (ii) Procedures that rate the extent to which the evaluatee has accomplished *job-targets* or performance objectives fixed to suit his needs. For this, various devices like interview schedules, check lists, questionnaire etc. are used to assess the effectiveness of supervision. Not only the supervisors, but also the subordinates and colleagues are given chances to express their views and share in the evaluation.

Neagley and Evans (p. 287) have rightly opined that all persons with supervisory roles should be evaluated by each other and by the classroom teachers. The check-lists may be used annually, but evaluation can and should take place at any time. If the proper climate of personal relationships and group interaction exists, staff-members learn to share successes as well as failures. Each person as he matures in this type of environment faces up to his own problems and does not blame someone else. On the other hand, credit is given where it is due. Evaluation then becomes an honest and fair assessment of the contribution of each individual to the instructional goals. With a number of persons involved, the total result should be helpful to the teachers and supervisors and to the programme of instruction.

However, to quote their own words, "Much research is needed in the development of more precise methods of evaluation". Probably, there will never be perfection in the measurement of relationships among human beings, but we should be able to discover more effective ways of assessing the contribution of each to the goal of better pupil learning experiences.

Evaluation Procedures in India: Inspecting officers in most of the States use proformas prescribed by the State Governments for inspection and supervision purposes. A few States like Kerala and Mysore have brought out comprehensive inspection manuals and codes for the use and guidance of inspecting officers. The inspection proformas include items like qualifications and suitability of leaching staff, standards of instruction, subject charts, time-tables, co-curricular activities, discipline of pupils, conditions of libraries and laboratories, conditions of school buildings and hostels, scale of fees, financial position of the institutions, constitution of managing committees, maintenance of registers and so on.

Primary school supervisor send the inspection proformas to the heads of schools one or two weeks in advance of the actual inspection in the States of Gujarat, Rajasthan, Tamil Nadu, Kerala, Andhra Pradesh and Karnataka (Mysore). In Maharashtra, the proformas are send one month in advance of the actual inspection. Assam, Bihar, Orissa, Punjab and Uttar Pradesh do not follow the practice of sending inspection proformas in advance to the heads of Primary Schools. Statistical information furnished in the proformas is checked by the inspecting officers at the lime of inspection. Some States follow the practice of sending their accountants to the schools well in advance of the actual inspection so that they can check the records etc. before inspection. Similarly, inspecting officers for secondary schools send inspection proformas to the heads of schools at least one or two weeks in advance of the actual inspection.

With a view to bringing about uniformity and balanced comprehensiveness in the inspection proformas, a scientific evaluation instrument for inspection and supervision is felt necessary. One such evaluative criteria has been developed by the NCERT and set as a model for State Governments. This is not of course, a perfect one, but the inspecting officers should have this before them. This is called "Supervision Proforma of Elementary Schools" consisting of a number of points on various aspects of school. Almost every aspect has three parts i.e. advance data, check list, and evaluation with commendation and recommendations. The Evaluative Criteria and the Evaluation Instruments for Inspection and Supervision of Primary and Secondary Schools developed by the NCERT are not yet widely adopted or adapted throughout the country. The State Institutes of Education in various States have already prepared such evaluative criteria for inspection and supervision. But they are yet to be used by the inspecting officers of the Department.

(B) Reporting of Supervision

The proforma when properly filled in and the data analysed and interpreted with scientific and objective commendations and recommendations, take the shape of reporting. Although most of the States have prescribed forms for reporting of inspection, the headings of the forms and points prescribed for the reports show a great variety. These forms are filled up beforehand or during time of inspection. In some States like Assam, Bihar, Orissa and Punjab, inspection reports are recorded on the inspection registers maintained by the schools.

Adequate reporting of the observation made during inspection is very important. As mentioned in a research paper by the author, (1973) "Inspection reports are the most fundamental and useful record and like mirrors they reflect the quality of supervision. The inspection reports also indicate the methods, comprehensiveness and frequencies of visits. From these evidences the effectiveness of supervision can be judged to a great extent."

After supervising a particular school, the inspecting officer takes an opportunity to discuss with the teachers individually and in the staff-meeting with a view to focussing their attention on the good and bad features observed. He should give his remarks so cautiously that the teachers would appreciate and accept them wilfully. His observations will inspire and stimulate, enlighten and encourage teachers. In the discussions, the supervisor will discuss encourage teacher. In the discussions, the supervisor will discuss the problems faced by the school faculty and the programme of the school. The shortcomings of the school are also pointed out to the teachers and headmasters in course of the discussions. The enlightened and resourceful inspecting officers bring to the notice of the school faculty the innovations and tested good practices prevalent in some other schools. Teachers are benefited by the superior knowledge, skill and expertise of the supervisor through discussion. On these occasions, the supervisor helps solving the problems of schools and extend necessary guidance to teachers. In an earlier research study, it is revealed that supervisors devoted a large part of their time discussing administrative problems. But it should be otherwise. It is very essential that supervisors should give guidance on all academic problems as they are the technical experts on the field.

Although opinions vary as to whether discussion should be made after or before or during supervision, it is beyond any controversy that discussion with teachers and school-committee members is an integral part of supervision. Dash and Parhi (1966, p. 14) have reported in a research study that 88 per cent of sub-inspectors referred to the discussion with the school committees and only 76 per cent of them said to have discussed with the teachers as well as in the staff-committee. In another study it is reportedly original (1969 p. 2) that 90 per cent of supervisor have mentioned to have discussed with teachers after supervision. 78 per cent before supervision and only 20 per cent during inspection. It is, of course, convenient and effective if discussion can be arranged after supervision as the supervisor will then be in a position to have a clear picture of the problems and teachers.

It is reported by the Study Group (pp. 22-23) on Supervision and Inspection that generally three copies of the inspection report are prepared by the inspecting officers of which one is sent to the school concerned for compliance, another to the senior officer concerned for information and review, while the third is retained in the office of the inspecting officer for follow-up and record. The time within which inspection reports are sent by the primary school inspecting officers to the schools and their management for compliance and to their higher officers for information and review, varies from State to State. In the States of Bihar, Orissa and Punjab, inspection reports are recorded in the inspection book/register maintained by the school on the day of inspection, immediately after the inspection is concluded. In Tamil Nadu, Andhra Pradesh and Uttar Pradesh also, inspection reports are written on the day of inspection. In Bihar, inspection reports are sent to the Senior Officers within a week, while in Assam, Rajasthan, Kerala, Tamil Nadu, Gujarat and Maharashtra, Primary School Inspecting Officers send inspection reports to the schools and their managements and also to their senior officers within a fortnight of the inspection. In Punjab, Block Education Officers submit the inspection reports to the concerned District Education Officers in regular monthly meetings. In Uttar Pradesh and Orissa also, inspection reports are submitted to the higher officers in about a months' time.

The Study Group mentioned above examined some of the inspection reports. It was found that in some cases inspection notes recorded by the inspecting officers tended to be sketchy. A few examples of such inspection notes are as follows: "there is scope for improvement of reading", "home-work not assigned regularly", "teaching of social studies not up to the mark" etc. Such superfluous remarks of the supervisors are neither helpful nor useful. This is the natural consequence of perfunctory inspection as criticized by the Mudaliar Commission and the result of "brief and flying visits" as reported in another study.

(C) Follow-up

Follow-up action on inspection reports is an important step that should not be neglected at all. Such follow-up of inspection remarks either by the inspecting officer himself or by other officers is extremely significant. But in a study report it was found that out of the 14 visits paid to a particular school only in one case mention has been made regarding such follow-up action. In case of another two schools this mailer has been referred to only or twice by the concerned inspecting officers. This is a very sorry state of affairs.

The Study Group of 1969 similarly have reported that the follow-up action on inspection reports in almost all the States, is usually checked by the inspecting officers at the time of next inspection. In Kerala, however, the inspecting officers keep a more constant touch with the schools in this regard. Cases of serious irregularities are reported by the inspecting officers to their higher authorities and also to the managing committees of private-aided schools in some States.

In such cases, accounts of the schools are got checked by special auditors. It is suggested that senior inspecting officers in course of their tours should check certain inspection reports given by junior ones for getting a clear idea about the methods, comprehensiveness and frequencies of inspection. They should also insist on the compliance activities and reports to that effect, on the part of teacher and school committee for implementing the suggestions of supervisors.

Due to unsatisfactory reporting and lack of proper follow-up action there is no adequate impact of supervision or desirable result of reporting of supervision. The research study referred to earlier has also reported that there was poor response of supervisors to the queries made as regards improvement as a result of reporting. Only 6 per cent of supervisors have reported that reporting brought about improvement in enrolment, in regular attendance, and 35 per cent in school improvement. This shows that the reporting has very little impact on the improvement of schools programmes or on the professional growth of the teachers. It is now time for the supervisors to evaluate their own work in the light of their experiences and plan their future work accordingly. They should make their reporting of supervision the real potential instrument for bringing about desired improvement in the teaching-learning situations as well as in the total school environment.

5

The School and Its Components

The Background

The etymological meaning of the term "school" is leisure. It has come from the Greek word "Skhole" meaning "leisure". The reason of associating leisure with school is attributed to the fact that in the ancient Greece education was available to those who had ample leisure at their disposal. The early Greeks were devoting their leisure hours mainly for self-improvement.

In the ancient times when mankind was in a primitive stage of development, education was in its simplest form. Life was then simple and easy. As it grew complex, education became sophisticated and formalised. As the social life was very simple, the family used to provide the child with all the activities and experiences that he needed for preservation and improvement of his life and culture. He was learning the vocations and life-patterns from the adults in the family, church, religious ceremonies, social functions and so on.

In course of time, however, the society became more complex and life more complicated; there was growth of human civilization and the quantum of knowledge and experiences enhanced. Consequently, the home or the family and other primitive agencies were found inadequate for transmitting the knowledge, skills and values i.e. the cultural heritage from one generation to another. Thus emerged a formal agency of education called the school.

The parents and other family members had to spend most of their time and energy in vocations or occupations and the children had to devote more time and attention to acquire sufficient knowledge and skills and to assimilate the cultural values for equipping themselves for their future life. Thus education of children became a specialised job or profession. The work of imparting education was handled by a group of persons who were learned and interested in the job of teaching others. These persons teaching children were called teachers.

The schools were established in all the civilized countries of the past i.e. India, China, Greece, Rome, Egypt and Babylonia. But schooling was mostly confined to liberal education only which included the teaching of language, philosophy, religion, arithmetic and so on. The children of rich, noble and priestly families were given that education and those from ordinary and low-class families were getting no formal education.

In our ancient land, the early Aryans settled along the river in beautiful and sylvan surroundings. They were leading a life of ease, simplicity and reflection about the natural and supernatural elements. Their education was mostly related to the satisfaction of basic physical needs and spiritual activities like worship and rituals. Such education was made available to children in the families. With the development of civilization, education became elaborate and formal as a result of which a separate group of persons called "Gurus" and different organisations like "Ashramas" and "Gurukuls" came into being. These seats of learning were situated in the natural surroundings "far from the madding crowd" and away from the "din and bustle of life".

The School and Its Components

In the beginning, the school had no separate entity. It existed in the homes of the Gurus, in the temples and churches and other places convenient to the local people. In the Buddhist times, schools were housed in the monasteries which were developed as centres of higher learning. Massive structures were constructed for the renowned universities like Nalanda, Taxila, Maktabs and Madrassas, used to impact Muslim education in the mosques or any other central religious places. Even in the European countries schools were housed in the Churches for long time. During the British period, schools were opened to provide Western education after the Wood's Despatch in 1854.

Consequent upon the outstanding advancement in science and technology, explosion of knowledge and skills in various subjects and fields, the traditional schooling with limited physical facilities was found to be quite inadequate. In modern times, the school had multifarious functions and duties to discharge-diversified courses, various programmes, practical activities, vocational subjects, ancillary services and so on. This necessitates a wide range of furniture, equipment, instruments, working space, seating and boarding accommodation. Big buildings and many personnel are felt necessary for housing and organising the academic and practical programmes as well as practices in the school.

School organisation and administration are gradually shifting from authoritarian to democratic trends. Attempts are being made to cater to the individual needs, interests, attitudes and aptitudes of both teachers and pupils. Adequate facilities are being provided for upliftment of latent talents and optimum growth of students in the emotional, psychological and physical aspects. With a view to achieving objectives of education, the school is required to be a big plant with its various components. The staff, the physical plant and the programmes and practices constitute various components-of the school.

The Staff

The staff of school may be divided into two categories: (1) teaching, and (2) non-teaching. The teachers including headmasters, laboratory assistants and librarians are broadly taken as teaching staff. The office assistants, peons, water bearers, sweepers etc. are called non-lasting staff. The size of the staff depends on the size and nature of the school. A school having 200 students will require a smaller staff than the school having 1000 strength. Similarly, a school having science and technological subjects must require a greater staff than the school providing only social sciences, languages and humanities.

The democratic organisation of the staff ensures its effective and efficient functioning, the spirit of cooperation, involvement and fellow-feeling usually facilitates the staff-working. The inter-personal relations and human interactions promote the effectiveness of the staff. A bright image of the school can be projected through maintenance of a high moral and a good professional standard in the staff. All the staff members should work in a team for realizing the objectives of the school.

It is called "teachers are the school". As a stream can never rise higher than its source, a school cannot rise above its teachers. Achievements of pupils and schools cannot be better than the teachers' capacities and performances. Of course it is said that pupils would not rise above the educational level of teachers, no social progress could be possible. But teachers must give intellectual, moral and social leadership to students and inspire them to make advancement in different fields according to their individual interests and aptitudes.

The Secondary Education Commission, 1952-53 has aptly said, "We are, however, convinced that the most important factor in the contemplated educational reconstruction is the teacher—his personal qualities, his educational qualification, his professional training and the place that he occupies in the school as well as in the community". (p. 126). The Commission has visualised the importance of the teaching personnel not only in the school, but also in the whole of community. Therefore it has added, The reputation of a school and its influence, on the life of the community invariably depend on the kind of teachers working in it. Priority of consideration must, therefore, be given to the various problems connected with the improvement of their status".

The Education Commission, 1964-65 have similarly mentioned, "Of all the different factors which influence the quality of education and its contribution to national development, the quality, competence and character of teachers are undoubtedly the most significant". (p. 46). The Commission therefore emphasizing significance of teachers' role in the national development in general and quality of education in particular has accorded highest priority on suitable recruitment and professional growth of teachers. It has observed, "Nothing is more important than securing a sufficient supply of high quality recruits to the teaching profession, providing them with best possible professional preparation and creating satisfactory conditions of work in which they can be fully effective (p. 46).

A qualified, competent and adequate staff is the main pre-requisite for the effective functioning of a school. Besides satisfactory service conditions and welfare services should be made available to teachers for ensuring a high standard of work. A poorly equipped and dissatisfied teacher instead of promoting, adversely affects the teaching-learning situations in the school. On the other hand, an efficient and satisfied teacher not only performs his allotted work adeptly, but also likes to implement a number of curricular as well as co-curricular programmes and encourages students in manifold activities for all-round development of their personalities and innate talents. A good teacher knows that learning is a cooperative venture and it becomes effective through mutual interacting of pupils and the teacher.

In-service education should be provided to all teachers in order to help them for updating their knowledge and skills. Unless teachers keep themselves abreast with the latest methods of teaching and subject-content, they cannot do justice to their duties and responsibilities. Therefore teachers have to grow always psychologically and intellectually. Since in our country most of the teachers are working in the rural areas, the need for in-service training programmes is imperative.

Teachers are to be assigned various responsibilities in organising curricular and co-curricular programmes according to their aptitudes and interests. Nobody should feel that he is overloaded with works, whereas nobody should feel that he is neglected. Work load should be uniform as far as possible. All staff members should be involved in the decision-making and planning process, so that everybody should be conscious of his share and role in organisation of the programmes. Initiative, freedom and responsibilities should go together.

Teaching duties are allotted to various members of the staff in two ways. If a teacher is made responsible for all subjects in a particular class, he is called a class teacher. If a teacher is entrusted with teaching the same subjects in several classes, he is called a subject teacher or specialist. Whether the system of class teacher is better than that of subjects teacher or vice versa is a thorny problem as much can be said on both sides. The following are the advantages in the specialist or subject teacher system:

(1) As the specialist teacher is confined to one subject only, he takes keen interest in the subject and tries to get comprehensive and deeper knowledge in that field.
(2) He gets time to conduct research, studies and experiments in the subject.
(3) Students have a chance of coming in contact with a large member of teacher and learning a variety of the things which widens their interest and outlook.
(4) Since the system introduces variety, it eliminates dullness and takes a long way in sustaining interest through the school day.
(5) The system also ensures a continuity of work or progress in a subject from class to class. The subject teacher teaches the same boys in the next class in his own field and makes use of the previous knowledge and background for making further progress or also making up the deficiency, if any.

Disadvantages in the subject teacher system are as follows:

(1) One of the dangers in the specialist system is that he is apt to shut himself off from the other members of the staff.
(2) Since he isolates his subject from others, his hatred and narrow mentality are developed towards other subjects.
(3) In this system, correlation and integration of various subjects as per the modern trend are not possible.

On the other-hand, the following advantages are cited in favour of class teacher system:

(1) The class teacher gets ample opportunities to know his children well and as such a psychological rapport is established between the teacher and the taught.
(2) He conducts more as a director than as an instructor. He is in a better position to act as a guide and to provide a congenial atmosphere for unfurling the latent talents.
(3) He is able to bring about correlation and integration of various subjects as a result of which narrowness is eliminated.

(4) Since one teacher is in-charge of a class and its activities, better coordination in progress and home assignment can be ensured which minimises the over burdening the students.

(5) The class feels greater responsibility for progress in the class as a whole.

(6) There is greater flexibility in the time-table for adjusting time to the subjects.

The disadvantages of the class teacher system are not far to seek. They may be mentioned as follows:

(1) The class teacher becomes the jack of all trades and master of none as he cannot get ample time for making a depth study of any particular subject.

(2) The class feels drudgery and dullness due to the presence of the same teacher there from the beginning to the end and lack of variety.

(3) Some subjects are likely to be neglected, as the class teacher may be interested in a few subjects and disinterested in others.

Although there are claims and counter-claims on both sides, it may be concluded that in junior classes like in Primary Schools, the system of class teacher is preferable to the other. Because the subject-content is not so much emphasized and correlation as well as integration among various subjects is felt more desirable at this stage. In higher classes, however, the subject teacher or specialist teacher system is preferred to the other as depth and comprehensiveness of the subject knowledge are laid a great stress. Some of the disadvantages of the class teacher system are reduced to the minimum by putting a teacher in-charge of a particular class and allowing him to teach the same batch of students in the very class upto a certain stage where depth of the subject has to be given importance.

Staff-Meetings

Staff-meetings should be held regularly at least once a month. All staff-members must attend these meetings. The real cooperative and academic spirit should prevail in them. The staff-meeting should be regarded as a common forum for mutual discussion and exchange of ideas. The difficult problems—curricular, co-curricular or administrative should be discussed in such meetings and decisions be taken for better solution.

The meetings should be democratically organised without any kind of authoritarianism or imposition from above. A secretary should be appointed for keeping the minutes and records of the proceedings. Although the headmaster should be in the chair for discussing administrative problems, subject specialists or faculty heads may preside the meetings for holding academic discussion or demonstration or presentation of an issue from the concerned subjects. It would be better to give sufficient notice of the meetings with important business or agenda, so that teachers will keep themselves free for the meeting and have time to think over the matters for discussion. Although it is not always possible to give sufficient notice for each meeting, attempts should be made to do that normally, The staff-meeting may also be held at the request of a reasonable number of staff-members. The staff-meetings properly organised will contribute to the professional growth of teachers.

6

The School Plant

The school plant is a comprehensive term meaning building, play ground, furniture, equipment, library, laboratory and so on. All the physical facilities that are required for achieving the various objectives of the school constitute the school plant. The school plant includes not only the existing facilities, but also the future requirements to meet the changing demands of education.

The school plant is the "child's home" during the school hours and the "community centre" afterwards. It may be called a "living laboratory" where children learn through living and doing. It is also known as a "youth centre" or a "civic enterprise" which provides recreational, educational, library and other cultural facilities for multifarious development and growth of the youths.

In this context, the following aspects may be considered for adequate and better provision of different facilities.

Planning

The important principles that may be kept in mind for provision of the school plant are as follows:

(1) The immediate as well as ultimate needs as required to realise the objectives of education at a particular stage and in a particular area should be clearly identified, formulated and phased according to urgency. That is why, both short-term and long-learn plans should be chalked out.

(2) This planning should ensure reasonable flexibility in order to facilitate necessary adjustments suiting to the changes that may occur in educational programmes in future.

(3) There should be sufficient room for additions and alterations in the school plant to accommodate changes in curriculum, roll-strength and personal.

(4) The trends of expansion in the local industries, commerce, communication and other ventures should be taken into consideration for planning the school plant.

(5) A "blue-print" or a master plan should be drawn up before starting any major construction work. This should provide all the present and future needs of the society.

The school plant should be functional, not ornamental. There must be wide-spread changes in curriculum, methodology, use of various instructional materials and so on. The American Association of School Administrators have laid down the following seven principles for planning the school plant.

1. *Curriculum adequacy* — The school plant should be adequate for organising curricular, co-curricular and community activities.
2. *Safety and well-being* — The school plant should protect comfort, health and safety of pupils and have adequate lighting, heating and ventilation.
3. *Inter-functional coordination* — Each unit or portion of a plant may be well-planned for its specific use, but if they are not properly coordinated, plant as a whole cannot be effective.
4. *Efficiency and unity* — The entire plant should be well-planned and well-designed to give unity and promote total growth, so that efficiency can be ensured.
5. *Beauty* — The school plant as a whole should be attractive, cheerful and pleasing.
6. *Adaptability* — The plant should be so designed that future adjustment to changing requirements will be possible without much difficulty or dislocation.
7. *Economy* — The school plant should not only be constructed

economically, but also be maintained and utilised for different purposes without much expenditure.

Site and Location

The importance of a suitable site and its location cannot be over-estimated. The site should be healthful and free from disturbing noise and odour. There should not be any danger for life and health from any natural and artificial elements in the local environment. Since the students spend their impressionable age at school, the school plant should be made beautiful and develop habits of cleanliness and healthful living.

The site of a school not be located in a congested area or at the heart of an industrial area. It should be accessible by different communication facilities and at the same time should be located in a quiet and pleasant environment. It should not be close to the market places, bus stand, railway station, burial or cremation ground, factory and stagnant pools. The school site should avoid water logging, muddy localities, rubbish heaps and unhealthy surroundings.

Area for the School Plant

Area is an important factor for selection of a site for the school. There is no hard and fast rule in this matter and it depends on the following points:

(i) *Strength of the school*: Since at least 10 square feet of floor space is necessary for a pupil, the area of a school will largely depend on its total strength of students.

(ii) *Nature of the school*: Residential schools must require larger areas than the day schools, as they must have additional space for hostel and staff quarters.

(iii) *Courses of studies*: The schools with teaching and working facilities in various technical, agricultural and animal husbandry subjects must require bigger areas than the schools providing only traditional and art subjects. That is why, at present schools are in need of more space for teaching so many work experience or socially useful productive work subjects.

(iv) *Co-curricular programmes*: With a view to organising various curricular programmes in the school a large area is necessary. For example, playground for games and sports, big area for gardening and so on are required to enable students to play, and to work in the garden.

Design and Dimensions

The Secondary Education Commission has said "Provision is made in such schools to see that there is free circulation of air, proper light, shelter for monsoons weather, and it is also laid down that the rooms constructed should have a minimum area to accommodate a certain number of school children in a class." (p. 158) The Commission opined that the number of students in any class should be limited so that class rooms are constructed to accommodate this number. But now-a-days this number has gone up and classes are over-crowded.

With a view to establishing personal contact between the teacher and the taught and to exert a wholesome influence on the pupil, the optimum number that should be admitted to any class should be 30 and the maximum should not exceed 40. As each pupil must be provided with more than 10 sq. ft. the minimum area of one room should be 500 sq. ft. A school with 500 pupils should have 10 sections and have 10 classrooms requiring 5,000 sq. ft. floor area. Besides, additional space should be provided for verandah, office, library, play ground, lavatory, agriculture, craft room etc. The larger the number of classes and sections and more subjects are provided in the curriculum, the larger has to be the area for classrooms and playground.

The School Building Committee of the Central Advisory Board of Education (CABE) has recommended the following minimum area:

No. of children	*Area of Building*	*Area of Play-ground*
160	½ acres	2-3 acres
320	1 acres	4-5 acres
480	1 ½ acres	6-7 acres

The school building should preferably be single-storeyed and have ample room for expansion in future. In case of hilly and densely populated areas, a two storeyed or even three storeyed building can be erected by way of expansion and extension.

The school buildings can be of several designs. Generally E, T, H, and U designs of buildings are popular as they are convenient and attractive. Different facilities like common rooms, conference hall or auditorium, library, visitors room officer room etc. should be provided in the same. The 'E' plan is said to be the best form of building in which rooms are open to the light, the hall is in a central position and two wings can easily be added to it. Sometimes when expansion is felt necessary a double 'E' form of building may be constructed, which is good and beautiful.

Ventilation and Lighting

Ventilation in class-rooms greatly influences comfort of pupils and teachers and efficiency of teaching-learning process. The ideal standard for circulation of air in a school building is 30 cubic feet of fresh air per minute per pupil. Ventilation of a room depends not only on air movement, but also on humidity and temperature. Therefore some safeguards are taken by making rooms spacious and airy with provision of many windows. Cross-ventilation and ventilators should be provided for free movement of air and exit of foul as well as intake of fresh air.

Temperature in a room is dependent on the relative humidity of air inside. When air is heated, relative humidity comes down. If moisture is not added to air when heated, evaporation of moisture from skin takes place rapidly. It becomes unbearable. Even in the rainy season when humidity of air goes up it becomes uncomfortable. It is stated for a room temperature of 70°F, the relative humidity should be 40 to 60 percent. In the winter when humidity goes below the standard, pupils feel more cold. The following suggestions have been given by I.P. Visa (1977) in this regard.

(i) Windows should be wire-gauged, so that even when they are opened, the wire-gauze may protect the room from dust and insects.

(ii) The height of windows should be about three feet above the floor. Windows should have ample width and height so that sufficient air and light come in.

(iii) There can be certain supplementary measures, e.g. ventilators for outlet of foul air and floor ventilators to admit fresh air from outside.

(iv) In a warm country like India, ceiling fans are necessary in every class-room. If fans move freely in summer and rainy season, over-perspiration, drought and suffocation can be considerably reduced.

Lighting should be adequate in the classroom which should be flooded with sunlight throughout the day. The light can come through windows and doors. The height of windows should be usually three feet from the floor, so that light falling on the pupil's desk is adequate. If the pupils sit on the floor, this height should not be more than two feet.

In this matter utmost precautions should be taken due to increased frequency of short-sightedness among pupils. Pupils cannot see distinctly the writing on the black board in less lighted rooms. The strain put on their eyes daily may badly affect their eyesight. Therefore the following measures may be adopted to ensure adequate lighting in the class-room.

(i) Classrooms and other rooms should be so designed that they do not face the sun at all times of the year, nor should they be deprived of light in any season. Therefore the building should face the south direction.

(ii) The rooms must have a large number of windows and doors to admit light from outside.

(iii) More light should come from left than from right, so that when the pupil writes, no shadow is cast on the paper.

(iv) Dazzling light should be avoided.

(v) Light should not shine on the faces of pupils, teachers or the black-board.

(vi) Coloured window panes should not be used as they obstruct light.

(vii) Walls should be white-washed and windows, doors or pillars may be coloured in light green or blue. Dark and crimson colours should be avoided.

(viii) There should be proper colour combinations in the equipment and furniture without presenting colour contrasts and glare.

(ix) Artificial lighting arrangement is necessary in the rooms without sufficient natural lighting.

Maintenance and Upkeep

Without proper maintenance even the most magnificent building and expensive equipment and furniture go waste. The headmaster should either himself attend to it or entrust this work to a vigilant staff-member. Since a stitch in time, saves nine, there should not be undue thrift in timely repair and maintenance.

The headmaster as the custodian of the school assets, should feel a sense of ownership or pride. He should take regular rounds and absence keenly the conditions of all rooms, equipment and furniture. Registers of maintenance and repairs of the school plant should be properly maintained.

Optimum Utilisation

Although the school plant, particularly building, is used for the educational purposes, community should also be allowed to use the same for village meetings, a wedding reception, elections, family planning etc. It is also suggested that school buildings should be used to the optimum by holding two independent schools in shifts or for the programme of non-formal education.

The Indian Education Commission, 1964-66 has aptly observed that since it is very costly to provide and maintain the physical plant of educational institutions, it becomes necessary to utilise it as fully as possible, for the longest time on each day and for all the days in the year by making suitable administrative arrangements. The laboratory, library, workshop, craftshed etc. should be utilised for at least eight hours a day. Institutional facilities may be utilised for community service, adult education and so on. Although it is evident from the Third Educational Survey, 1979 that the community participation in the school activities is greater than the school participation in the community activities, the position in fact is not encouraging. It has been emphasized in a study (1980) that for democratisation and improvement of education, such cooperation and collaboration should be promoted between the school and the community.

The Special Rooms

In addition to the class rooms for teaching subjects of general nature, a number of special rooms for teaching some important specific subjects like Science, Geography, SUPW subjects like Domestic Science, Music, Craft etc. is found useful. The need for the special rooms is felt more at present than earlier due to modern educational theory and changes in the syllabus. The special rooms also help in creating an atmosphere congenial; to the nature and scope of the subjects concerned. Much of the time and energy is also saved by teaching the subject in the special room and utilising all the necessary equipment, apparatus, and other aids without moving to another room and without asking anybody else to bring the same. It is risky to take not only breakable and delicate materials from one room to another, but also durable objects are defaced and mishandled if moved from one class room to another. Hence special rooms are found conducive to teaching the subjects concerned under favourable conditions.

The special rooms which are important under the present conditions are discussed below.

The Science Room

A special room is essential for effective teaching science and the science room should have three parts:

(1) A science/lecture theatre,
(2) A science laboratory, and
(3) A store-room.

In the elementary school, all these three parts may be combined in one room. Even one or two almirahs will suffice for safe upkeep and custody of the valuable equipment.

A big table should be kept in one fixed position for class work and another for laboratory work. Gas, electricity and water connections should be available to this room. The size of the science room is determined by the number of students using the room at a time. For example, the size of a science room should be 48’ × 25’ for a class of 40 boys in demonstration and 20 boys in laboratory work. The front part may be used for demonstration and the hind part for practicals. There should be 2 long wall black boards, one in each part of the room. The demonstration part should be provided with tables and chairs for boys and a long table for demonstration by the teacher. The other part should be furnished with practical tables. There should be three sinks in the room one for the teachers and another for the pupils. There should be adequate number of almirahs for storage purposes. Everything should be cleaned and oiling of the machines should be done regularly. After each experiment, the apparatus should be cleaned and dried and kept in its place.

One of the important feature of the science room is the Museum where natural and scientific specimens and models can be kept. The exhibits may consist of leaves, flowers, seeds, birds, insects, skeletons of animals, shells, nests, fruits, roots, ores, weeds, charts. A cup board, a few shelves or almirahs with glass fronts should be used for arranging them systematically and properly labelled.

The Social Sciences/Studies Room

With a view to creating social climate and making all necessary equipment and aids available in a room, a special room for teaching social sciences or social studies is felt useful. In this room a wall chalkboard, a bulletin board and various audio-visual materials like maps, charts, graphs, pictures, models, specimens, films, slides, radio sets, (television set if available), tape-recorder etc. should be properly preserved and used whenever there are classes. A library may also be kept for ready reference. Some show-cases, a few cup boards, some shelves and two or three almirahs should be used for storage and display. There need not be any separate room for history or geography teaching. This room can fruitfully be utilised for the purpose.

Art and Craft Room

Arts and crafts have found an important place in the modern school curriculum. A separate room provided with adequate number of tables, chairs, storage facilities, stands for apparatus and equipment is found helpful for these activities like toy-making, modelling, woodwork, embroidery, painting and drawing.

This room should not be crowded and wash basins as well as sinks should be fitted in the room for cleaning. A teacher's demonstration table may be placed at a central place and all kinds of apparatus necessary for different activities should be kept properly.

Home Science/Domestic Science Room

Previously, home science or domestic science was only an optional subject meant for girl students. But under the new curriculum as a subject under socially useful productive works, it has acquired special importance. Its scope has also been widened and now it encompassed instructions in simple cookery laundry, dietics, child care, hygiene, decoration and furnishing. The equipment for home science room include electric heaters, gas stoves, a coal range with ovens, sinks for hot and cold water, refrigerator, electric irons, tables, sewing machines, crockery, utensils, pots, tables for preparing food, wash basins and storage facilities. Thus the entire will have three parts i.e. (i) the workshop, (ii) kitchen, and (iii) the store. Although for proper maintenance of the room and equipment, there will be servants and menials, the teacher concerned and the students should take personal interest in the matter.

The Assembly Hall/Auditorium

The Assembly Hall is a multipurpose room and can be used for different programmes. It can be used for morning assembly, dramatics, debates, public lectures, symposia and film-shows. Hence this room serves the purpose of an auditorium. It can serve as gymnasium, an audio-visual room, a reading room and a refreshment room. Last but not the least, the Assembly Hall provides facilities of a community centre.

Therefore, size of the Hall should be quite spacious with all the facilities of a public hall. It should not be less than 40' × 60'. The Hall should be so located that there is access to all sides and no disturbance from any side. As far as the internal-arrangement is concerned, some special measures should be taken to make it more convenient and useful. There should be a big stage with green rooms on its both sides. There should be a permanent arrangement of seats, so that a programme can be organised with a short notice. The walls of the hall should be decorated with photographs, oil-paintings of greatmen, previous teachers of distinction, reputed educationists and beautiful scenery. Lastly, there should be adequate ventilation and lighting arrangement.

Library Room

Library is an indispensable part of the school. It has been the centre of modern educational activities for organising seminars, symposia, project works, in-service training course and so on. There should be a reading room adjacent to the library and a large number of seats, desks, book shelves and almirahs with artistic effect for making it pleasant and attractive. There should be sufficient provision for light and air. The library should be conveniently located with easy access to all pupils of various classes and all teachers of the school.

Modern library is not merely a place for locating books and journals in the advanced educational institutions in the West. It is called a "learning resources centre" which provides different kinds of audio-visual media and materials including slides, film-strips, educational films, radio and TV programmes. That is all kinds of facilities and resources are made available in the centre for promoting learning experiences. The library room in our country should be planned accordingly with a vision for the future growth and development.

Office Room

The office room is the nerve-centre of the school and successful organisation of various school programmes largely depends on the efficiently functioning of the office. It should be well-equipped and provided with adequate facilities like type-writers, duplicator, almirah, shelves etc.

The office room should be centrally located and the headmaster's room should be adjacent to it. It should be accessible to all students, teachers, guardians and officials. Besides, a waiting room should be situated close to the office room for enabling visitors to wait there comfortably.

The Hostel and its Superintendent

Although importance of the school hostel has gone down with the expansion of schools in the nook and corner of the country, it is regarded as a centre of citizenship training and second home of the pupils. Many good qualities of head and heart are developed at the hostel. The hostel should be provided with adequate sanitary facilities. It is desirable to set up a single-storied building for the hostel. The superintendent's quarters should preferably be attached to the hostel.

The Hostel should not be treated merely as a place for boarding and lodging of the pupils. It should provide all the opportunities for promoting healthy habits and developing good qualities like fellow-feeling, cooperation, mutual help, punctuality. The hostel life should cater to the needs of the future citizen by providing ample opportunities for civic training.

The superintendent sometimes known as the warden is chosen from among the staff members. He should be democratic minded and work as the philosopher and guide of the inmates. He should have parental love and affection towards children of the hostel. He should be professionally and academically well-equipped to guide the inmates successfully. His sociability, sympathy, understanding, sincerity, broad-mindedness and impartiality must win confidence as well as regards from the students. He must be a man of character and vision.

The warden should pay frequent visits to the physical, academic and living facilities and ensure proper functioning of various mechanisms and agencies involved in the hostel administration. The inmates should be encouraged to share hostel administration and decision-making, so that they will be trained in democratic management and community living.

Equipment and Furniture

In many State, the Education Departments or the Boards of Secondary Education have developed their education codes and lists of minimum equipment and furniture for different stages of education. This has been done with full realisation that without these minimum facilities education cannot be efficient and effective. These are also necessary from the health point of view and for convenience as well as comforts that are badly required for making education attractive and interesting. Adequate care and precautions should be taken for providing suitable equipment and furniture, otherwise instead of promoting, they will stand on the way of better teaching-learning process.

The Secondary Education Commission have said to have noticed many schools where there was hardly equipment and subjects were taught under conditions where boys were forced to memorise rather than understand what was taught. The Commission have also felt that the laboratories were hardly ever used, except as store-houses for odds and ends; theoretical instruction in such important subjects as Physics and Chemistry was given in the class room. Geography is said to have been taught without maps, Physics without models and instruments and Chemistry without rudiments of a laboratory.

Therefore all attempts should be made for providing suitable equipment and furniture and also for optimum utilisation and maintenance. All the class-room equipment may be divided into two categories: (1) Essential, and (2) Desirable.

1. Essential Equipments

(1) Desks and chairs for the pupils or matting on the floor.
(2) Black board or chalkboard either on a wall or resting on an aisle.

(3) A chair and a table for the teacher.
(4) A map-stand and a pointer.
(5) A few chalks and a duster.

2. Desirable Equipments

(1) An almirah or a big cupboard carved into the wall for keeping books.
(2) A notice board, a bulletin board.
(3) Ceiling fan and artificial light.
(4) Drinking water in the jars or buckets.
(5) Some relevant illustrations, models, specimen and other A.V. materials.

Furniture and equipments are important and greatly affect the physical, mental, emotional development of children. P.C. Wren writing about this has rightly remarked, "Furniture plays and extremely important part in the physical, moral and mental welfare of scholars. If the desks be of the wrong kind, or if benches be used instead of desks, curvature of the spine, contraction of chest, roundness of the shoulders and a confirmed stoop may result as physical injury; bad discipline irritation, discount and discomfort may result as moral injury and inability to sustain attention and concentration owing to lack of bodily case may result as mental injury."

But it is experienced that neither the headmaster nor the management realizes the importance of the right type of furniture. Far from furniture, even the floor without any matting is used for seating of the pupils in most of the primary schools. Wherever there are chairs and desks, they are not of the right size. There are backless and deskless benches in a number of secondary schools. The students sitting there continuously, develop very bad postures affecting their eyesight and spinal cord adversely. The desks and benches are also often so much fixed and dumped that pupils have to observe only one posture throughout the day and feel discomfort both physical and mental due to lack of flexibility. It is necessary that the pupils' legs should be free to move and they should have flexibility in sitting and standing.

Desks and Benches

The height of the desks and seats should also be according to the age and height of the pupils. Therefore the height must vary from school to school—primary, middle or high. The seat should not be so high that the legs do not reach the floor and remain hanging.

The seats also should not be so low to force legs stretching in slanting position beneath the desk. There should not be any pressure under the knee. The height of the back of the seat should not press the neck. The height of the writing surface of the desk should allow the child to sit erect with ease and the arm should rest on the desktop comfortably. The sitting space on the chair should be adequate enough for permitting free movement of legs. The top surface of the desk should not be flat, but must have a slope of 15 degrees.

The relative position of seat and desk is shown by three illustrations:

(i) Plus position,
(ii) Zero position, and
(iii) Minus position.

In the plus position there is a positive distance between the seat and the desk. In the zero position, the vertical line from the inner edge of the desk exactly meets the inner edge of the seat. In the minus position, the seat is thrust inside the space beneath the desk i.e. the distance between the seat and the desk in minus. It is advised that the minus position should be avoided. The zero position is suitable for writing and the plus position is suitable for reading as well as standing.

Seats should not be fixed with the desks, so that the pupil can easily move his seat a little back or front in order to stand erect. The plus position can be artificially created by providing fixed seat-cum desks. The maximum length of each desk should be twelve feet. But it is desirable as it restricts free movement of pupil.

Dual desks are to be preferred to long desks. Each pupil should be provided at least 18 inches of sitting space. Gangways of 18 inches may be left between the desks and walls. The rows of desks should be arranged at right angles to the window wall.

Black Board or Chalk Board

Black board has been the most simple, but very useful teaching aid in the class room. Although it is a very traditional equipment being used for the entire class for demonstrating, for teaching and for writing as well as drawing on, it is now found in various types and colours. According to differences in mechanism used, there are at least four types:

(1) The wall black board means a painted area of the wall being used for writing purposes.
(2) The framed wall board is a wooden board fixed on the walls through hooks.
(3) The sliding wall board which rests on pulleys and is movable up or down.
(4) The black board that rests on an easel.

Each type of black board has its own merits and can be used under the existing limitations. The wall black board is the most economical one and can be provided in each room from the very beginning of construction. It provides ample space for writing and drawing on. But its disadvantages are: it cannot be moved and may not be visible to the back benchers due to glare abstracting eyesight. The sliding blackboard can be easily moved up and down and writing on one black board can be concealed for test purposes. But it is comparatively costlier and requires technical know-how for preparation. The framed as well as hooked wall board is not convenient for use. Rather the black board on the easel is the best for use and economical in preparation. It is mobile and can be used in any place and in any manner according to convenience.

The black board should be placed conveniently, so that writing is seen by everybody in the class and the light does dazzle on writing. The black board should not be placed near a window obstructing light. But it should be located on the left-hand side of the teacher at an inclination of 45 degrees with the class. It should be placed very near the teacher's dais or his table so that it can be used conveniently. The height of the black board above the floor should vary from 25 to 40 inches. The height can be adjusted on an easel. The size of the black board may be 4 feet into 2½ feet.

In primary schools a black board railing 2 feet high above the floor on all sides of the room can be prepared for facilitating children's writing on it at their will. Black or green colour is found best for painting the chalk board and varnishing it should be done regularly after reasonable intervals. The surface should not be glossy, otherwise the eyesight of pupils may be adversely affected.

Wet dusters should be used for cleaning the black if blackboards are washed daily before and after the school hours. Although white chalks are preferred to other chalks, coloured chalks may occasionally be used for special purposes. There should be cup-boards in every room for keeping chalk pieces and duster.

Cup-Board and Almirah

A cup-board or an almirah in every class room is essential for storing chalk-box, duster, map, globe, pointer, attendance and other registers. A few reference books, library books, charts, models, pictures, posters etc. should be kept there for use in the class rooms. The cup-board or almirah should be kept away from insects and cleaned of dusts regularly. The cup boards should be constructed into the wall and preferably be glass fronted.

Teacher's Chair and Table

The teacher's place for sitting and delivering his lesson should be fixed conveniently, so that it will be possible on his part to supervise the entire class and glance over the activities on the students. It is preferable to have a raised dais or platform for the purpose. P.C. Wren has rightly remarked, "The teacher's table or desk and chair should always be upon a dais raised to one foot or eighteen inches above the floor level to enable him to see the desk surface before each boy in the class."

Audio-Visual Media and Materials

With a view to making the teaching-learning process effective, various audio-visual media and materials are used by teachers at different stages of education. Educators in the advanced countries are utilising and developing new material to make education meaningful and interesting. The use of A.V. materials in our teaching-learning situation is not at all satisfactory. The research studies conducted on the impact of A.V. materials on education have shown that knowledge, thinking, understanding, attitude and skills are improved by the use of A.V. aids. It is also evident that students of all categories whether bright or dullard gain from the usc irrespective of their age and grade levels.

The audio-visual materials are divided into three categories: (i) visual, (ii) audio, and (iii) audio-visual. The materials which appeal only to sight are of the first category. Examples of these materials are slides, film-strips transparencies, silent/motion pictures and projections with opaque and overhead projectors. Other materials traditionally, used in the schools are textbooks, illustrations, prints, graphs, charts, maps, globs, posters etc. which may be taken as visual aids. The chalk boards, felt boards, bulletin boards are also visual materials appearing only to the sense of sight. Displays, exhibits like specimens, models, electric maps, diagrams and dramatisations like puppetry, pantomimes, dancing etc. are regarded as successful visual materials.

Radio, tape-recorders, gramophones and different magnetic recordings provide audio materials which are appealing to the ear only. The television programmes, video tape recordings and films are audio-visual materials which appeal both sight and sound. Dramatic plays, role-playing, socio-drama etc., are a few types of dramatisation that can be utilised in education with a great success.

These three types of materials audio or visual or audio-visual, cannot be exclusively classified. There is no compartmentalisation and the list of such materials is not exhaustive. Imaginative and resourceful teachers can invent, explore and discover various sources of collecting and developing these materials. I.S. Kinder (1959) has rightly observed, "Any device which can be used to make the learning experience more concrete, more realistic, more dynamic can be considered audio-visual material."

The following guiding principles may be considered for effective utilisation of A.V. material:

(1) No one type of material should be used to the exclusion of others that is, in using one medium or, materials, others may be used for support. For example, for effective utilisation of radio, programmes, printed materials like teachers' notes and graphics like illustrations, slides may be used with profit.
(2) Certain materials seem more appropriate than others for teaching some objectives or units.
(3) Too much materials should not be used at a time as they may confuse rather than clarify the concepts.
(4) Preparation for the use of these materials should be made earlier.
(5) The pupils should be encouraged to actively participate in the process of utilisation.
(6) Materials should never be used haphazardly nor work periods allowed to become more entertainments.
(7) instructional materials, teaching methods and on objective of education should be coordinated and well-integrated.

The proper utilisation of A.V. materials calls for planning and organisation of resources adequately and appropriately. Besides, utmost care should be taken for maintenance and upkeep of the audio-visual materials media which are expensive as well as delicate.

7

The School Activities

In this chapter school activities which are co-curricular in nature have been described. Previously these activities were regarded as extra curricular and so much emphasis was not given on organising the same. But of late, attitude towards these activities has changed and all-round development of the child has been the goal of education. Besides intellectual, physical, emotional, ethical, social, aesthetic and cultural development is to be aimed at and ancillary activities need to be organised in the schools as the media of self-expression and means of personality growth. The Secondary Education Commission, 1952-53 has therefore forcefully observed "putting the problem in these words obviously, we do not visualise this school as merely a place of formal learning, whose main concern is to communicate a certain prescribed quantum of knowledge, but rather as a living and organic community which is primarily interested in training its pupils in what we have called, the gracious "art of living" knowledge and learning are undoubtedly of value but they must be acquired as a by-product of interested activities because it is only that they can become a vital part of the student's mind and personality and influence his behaviour."

Advantages of Co-curricular Activities

The values of co-curricular activities are multifarious and important from educational points of view. The various advantages of these activities may be discussed under the following heads:

The Physical Advantages

There are many co-curricular activities like games, sports, athletics, scouting, dancing, hiking etc. which are helpful for the growth and development of the body. Many activities provide healthful channels for the superfluous energy of the pupils, they also contribute to the sound, health, physical development, vital powers, healthful habits, vocational efficiency and personal happiness.

Most of the co-curricular activities have immense psychological values. There are many strong instincts in the adolescents and unless they are sublimated, these instincts create a large number of psychological problems. For example, the gregarious instinct less directed to fruitful tasks through self-government, community work, social service and other group works, might find its expression in student unrest, gang activities and other anti-social activities. All the instincts of self-assertion, self-abasement, curiosity, constructiveness, acquisitiveness, sex and gregariousness find desirable expressions through these co-curricular activities. Rather these activities play an important role in training emotions. All these plays are called cathartic in nature as they purge out the pent up emotions. Even the most dullards in the class rooms who are suppressed due to inferiority complex find outlets to their emotions in the play-ground and the most notorious boy wins many prizes in the sports and games. The engagement in these activities is also found conducive to their sound mental health.

Academic Value

Every academic programme should have two aspects: (i) theoretical and (ii) practical. Most of the classroom activities today are theoretical in character. Unless they are supported as well as supplemented by practical activities, the learning experiences will be lop-sided. Co-curricular activities provide practical experiences adequately. For example, theoretical discussion in geography, social studies science and language studies can be supplemented by learning experience through excursions, library activities, nature study field trips and hiking. Similarly, civics will be more meaningful and lively if activities like elections for self/students government, more assembly. Mantri Sabha etc. can be organised in the school effectively.

Social Value

Most of the school activities have social implications. Through the activities which are mostly cooperative in nature call for social traits like cooperation, mutual help, understanding, fellow-feeling, tolerance and sharing responsibility. Pupils learn these traits very easily. They acquire group loyalty—loyalty to the school, loyalty to the family, loyalty to the nation and loyalty to the world. The specific social activities which provided social training are scouting, girls' guide, Red Cross, community work, social service camps etc. The school should be regarded as a true replica of the society and all the activities relating to adults' life should be organised in the school.

Aesthetic Value

It is essential to promote a sense of beauty and appreciation in the pupil. To develop artistic sensibility i.e. aesthetic attraction to beauty—beauty in himself, beauty in the home, beauty in the school or beauty in the environment in general is one of the objectives of education. But aesthetic sensibility cannot be learnt through textbooks or speeches, it has to be learnt in life activities, in habits and in conduct. It cannot be taught, it is to be caught. That is why, school should provide adequate opportunities for developing sense of beauty and artistic outlook. Drawing, painting, decoration, toy-making, clay modelling, preparation of charts and models not only express, but also develop aesthetic sensibility in the children. Besides, ears of students can be trained to appreciate the musical sound and rhythm in music, dance, cultural shows, variety entertainment and so on. All these promote aesthetic values in education.

Recreational Values

Modern culture is evaluated by the criteria of leisure time activities. It is said that one's culture is known by the way his leisure is used. Unless the students are taught how to utilise their leisure most usefully, they cannot contribute to cultural growth satisfactorily and enjoy their life to the optimum. On the other hand they may engage themselves in anti-social activities and waste their time and energy in gossiping, gambling, wandering aimlessly, reading obscene books and visiting ugly pictures. Therefore, students should be encouraged to participate in arts, music, dance, symposia, debates, discussions, exhibitions, games, sports and other hobbies, so that they can learn the methods and means of utilising their leisure through recreational and creative activities.

Thus the co-curricular activities can effectively promote the all-round development of the child through sublimation, enjoyment, recreation, emulation, socialisation and academic growth. Without them the school is lifeless, teachers are machines, pupils are book works and education is one-sided.

General Guidelines for Organising Activities

1. Activities should be properly integrated with the curricular work.
2. Adequate planning and scheduling of the activities should be done in time.
3. Provision should be made for necessary equipment, accommodation, furniture and other contingencies.
4. Duties for organisation of different activities should be equitably distributed among the staff members.
5. Activities should also be allotted to the individual members of the staff according to their interest, aptitude and attitude.
6. Activities must be distributed properly throughout the year and each activity must have its rightful place in the schedule.
7. They must be organised in accordance with the ideals and image of the school.
8. Expenditure should be economised as far as possible without any useless and undesirable items
9. Organisation of activities should not be just a show work or window-dressing as some headmasters organise some selected activities, only to attract attention of the public and officials.
10. Proper recording of activities with the help of written and visual media should be made without delay.

Limitations and Usual Defects

In organising the school activities a large number of defects and difficulties are experienced which tell upon the good effects and purposes of the programmes. They may be mentioned as follows:

(1) *Lack of Facilities:* Many programmes cannot be properly organised without adequate facilities, suitable furniture, appropriate equipment and trained personnel. Even many activities which have to be organised as part of the curriculum are only accorded with lip-sympathy and without any sincere efforts. For example, recently socially useful productive work has been provided in the curriculum, but no adequate provision has been made in the school. Hence proper organisation of these activities has been an exception than a rule.

(2) *Lack of Pupils' Participation:* All activities in the school should be democratically organised from planning to evaluation. But in most of the schools this kind of involving pupils from the very beginning is ignored and consequently, the students do not feel belongingness and interest in the activities. That is why, they have to be motivated and associated with the work at various phases.

(3) *Over Expensive Show-off:* Sometimes for organising activities in the school, the students are asked to bring costly equipment like musical instruments, costly dresses, tape recorder etc. To make a great show-off, inviting VIPs, great dignitaries and arranging very expensive paraphernalia the over-enthusiastic headmasters and teachers spend a lot and collect a big amount from pupils. On account of this, pupils are unnecessarily in trouble and their enthusisation is flagged.

(4) *Defective Scheduling or No Scheduling:* The activities are often scheduled wrongly or no scheduling is made for various activities. Since no periods are provided or if provided not in_right time, activities are organised without any pre-planning and necessary preparation. So they are done haphazardly without achieving the desired objective.

(5) *Over-emphasis on Academic Work:* As present examination

is over emphasized and academic aspects are over estimated, schools are more interested in percentage of pass and winning onwards or ranks, than in organising suitable activities for improving the personality and talents of children. Since special interest is taken by everybody in academic matters, activities, even of interesting nature are ignored.

(6) *Over-emphasis on Activities:* Opposite trend is evident in certain schools where more emphasis laid on activities than an academic programmes. Over-enthusiastic headmasters and teachers take immense interest in organising a large number of activities through the year as a result of which too much time and energy is devoted to preparation only. They, for example, spend months together for staging a drama or organising sports tournament or celebrating the Annual Day of the School. The students who are interested in these activities spend all their time and energy on them entirely neglecting their studies.

(7) Another difficulty is experienced in a few schools where the over-ambitious and fastidious headmasters emphasize not only the academic programmes, but also co-curricular activities. Consequently the students as well as teachers are overworked and fail to do justice to any work. This leads also to dissatisfaction, frustration back-biting and leg-pulling.

Unless these difficulties are taken care of, by adequate pre-planning, balancing both the curriculum and co-curricular activities and proper distribution of the work load among the staff members, the very purpose of activities cannot be served and the objectives will be left unrealized.

The School Assembly

It is a good practice in the progressive school to begin the days work with a morning assembly. On this occasion, the entire school population assembly for a common prayer and then talks from the headmaster or from other teachers. This prayer should be general in character without any denominational reference. Besides prayer songs, some patriotic songs may be recited. This occasion is also utilised for making announcements regarding the day's programme particularly competitions, celebrations, time-table. Here the students get themselves familiar with the rules, regulations, ideals and practices of the school and thus are acquainted with the community spirit and image of the school. Some students and teachers take the opportunity to announce the local, regional, national as well as international news.

The school assembly is regarded as a means of controlling and directing the efforts and activities of pupils as a whole. It serves as a common forum and a clearing house for motivation how to behave in public meetings, to get accustomed to be speakers as well as audience which is a kind of citizenship training.

The school assembly in order to be effective should be properly planned and organised. Teachers and pupils should cooperate in planning and organising the assembly. The agenda of the assembly should not be traditional and stereotyped. It should be lively, meaningful and motivating.

There should be adequate discipline and orderliness. No gossiping and talking, no abusive remarks should be allowed. Reprimanding or sermonising here should also be avoided. The assembly should be a source of inspiration and enlightenment. The headmaster's presence and active interest in this will help making it successful.

Debates, Discussions, Seminars and Symposia

With a view to promoting expression and intellectual powers, debates, discussions, seminars and symposia should be organised in the school adequately. These activities provide pupils with the opportunities of collecting information organising ideas, presenting facts, speaking effectively and conducting before the audience properly. The pupils get confidence and speak with presence of mind, learn oratory or art of elocution through participation in these activities.

Such activities should also be properly organised in order to be effective, the teacher interested in these matters should be kept in-charge of planning and organising these activities. Topics for discussion or debate should be scheduled and publicised earlier. The number of speakers, their names, place, date and time for holding the debates should be announced as early as possible. The teacher should also give students necessary guidance for making preparations by consulting books and reference materials. The topics selected for discussion should be of current importance and thought-provoking. Cramming and using obscene and abusive language should be discouraged. Pupils should be encouraged to participate in large number and nobody should be discouraged in any way.

Although the format of debates, panel discussion, seminars and symposia are different from one another, the main objective is to train pupils to speak effectively, present facts interestingly and behave in the public meetings courteously. This objective is also closely related to citizenship training which a pre-requisite for success of democracy.

Dramatics

Dramatics is a playful activity in which both creative expression and artistic imitation combine. As the pupil plays varied roles, he satisfies his internal urge to play and to imitate. Through this activity he expresses himself and finds enjoyment. It therefore helps maintaining his mental health and as such it is of great therapeutic value. It provides opportunities for the release of pent up emotions, for improving speech and other qualities of elocution. Pupils may be encouraged to write their plays on the topics in textbooks. It helps them to improve their literary ability and to get themselves acquainted with various subjects like music, staging, decorating and so on. Even the pupils who act as audience are benefited to a great extent and besides entertainment learns many facts from history, geography, sociology and their life experiences described in the dramatics.

Dramatics are of different kinds. Students may stage a full-length drama written by a distinguished author. It is expensive as well as time-taking. Hence it is desirable to stage one-act plays which are of smaller duration. Dance drama is another variety of dramatics where the whole theme is expressed through dance and music. Pantomime is a form in which everything is expressed through action without speech. A puppet play is a type of dramatics in which puppets play different characters of a play. A person skilfully play the roles of various characters in a histrionic. A play or an episode or a feature can be represented through a series of pictures, scenes and other visuals only. It is called a pageant. Radio play is a modern variety of dramatics in which students can play different characters through voice and sound effects only. Now-a-days it has become very popular with students and many schools have displayed their interest and proficiency in this programme.

Dramatics should be properly organised and teachers having interest and experience in dramatics should be entrusted with this actively. As many pupils as possible should be encouraged to participate in this activity. Full-fledged dramas should be staged only on special occasions like annual days, centenary celebration etc. But one act plays and variety shows should be organised and pupils should be given various responsibilities for organising such activity.

Boy Scouting and Girl Guide

Scouting is meant for the boys in the age-group from 11 to 18. Every scout takes a solemn oath to obey the Scout Law which consists of ten rules relating to honour, loyalty, obedience, friendliness, courteousness, cheerfulness, usefulness, thrift and cleanliness. He puts on a special uniform and learns the use of ropes and sticks, learns first aid and social service, organises camp fires and field trips, learns to lead a camp life and to live a corporate life and gets himself trained to leaden independent life, but with team spirit. The girl-guide, on the other hand, learns activities like cooking, nursing, singing, dancing, drill, social service and first aid.

Scouting and girl-guiding are useful in many respects. Firstly, it promotes the physical health of the pupils through a series of physical activities. Secondly, it contributes to the mental health of the students through a large number of pleasing and joyful activities. Thirdly, it appeals the emotions and interest of the adolescents. It sublimates instincts of curiosity, assertiveness, adventure and gregariousness. It promotes the spirit of adventure through camping, hiking and outdoor life. It trains their emotions and provides catharsis through camp fires, shouting slogans and fights. It develops aesthetic sensibility and love for the nature.

Fourthly, it gives them practical skills in fighting against fire, using stick and knife, tying knots, pitching tents which are found useful in life. Beside many useful lessons in first aid, nursing, carpentry, kitchen gardening are also quite helpful in day-to-day life. Fifthly, scouting and guiding promote a large number of good qualities of head and heart like perseverance, thrift, loyalty, cheerfulness, obedience, patience, observation, patriotism, discipline etc., which are essential for success in life. Sixthly, through camp life and cooperative activities the boys and girls get social training. The ideals of citizenship, cooperation, mutual help follow-feeling are better practised and the scouts as well as guides render all possible social services with great efficiency.

Scouting and guiding should be properly organised in the school. The teachers having training and interest in the work should be entrusted with the organisation and students with favourable attitude and aptitude towards these activities should be selected for the purpose. All the materials and equipment like first-aid box, camping requirements, budges, uniforms, ropes, knifes, sticks etc. should be collected from the beginning. Adequate opportunities should be provided for camping as well as rendering community services. Proper recording and evaluation of all these works should be made systematically.

Literary Activities

The literary activities are useful means of promoting creative writing and self-expression they help in publicising the school activities and moulding the future writers of the society. Literary society may be formed and literary meetings should be held on the occasions of the birth days, death anniversaries of novelists, poets, dramatists such meetings may be made more lively and useful by inviting distinguished authors. School/class magazines, wall magazines, bulletins, school calendars should be prepared and published by the literary society from time to time. The literary activities also largely influence the quality and standard of academic performance.

The outcomes of these activities depend much on the success of organising them. The teachers having literary interest and ability should remain in-charge of organising these activities. The headmaster should also take active interest in the programme and encourage the students and teachers in literary activities, so that they can contribute to the development of literature and help projecting a bright image of the school.

Athletic Activities

Sports, games and athletics should be organised in the schools in order to help pupils in the conservation of their health, development of health habits, promoting their personality, team spirit and so on. Athletic activities help developing all-round personality of the pupils and train in citizenship qualities. That is why, play ground is called the cradle of democracy.

But at present these activities are not properly taken care of and facilities for organising them are quite inadequate. Teachers are also still under the impression that giants in athletics are dwarfs in academic matters and vice versa which is now exploded as a blind myth. The Secondary Education Commission has observed that these activities should be emphasized and the dearth of facilities should be made up with the community help.

With a view to organising the athletic activities properly, a schedule of the sports and games and of participation of each team by rotation should be drawn up from the beginning. Necessary equipment and materials for various sports should be provided by the school. A teacher interested in the programme should be in-charge of the activities. Adequate guidance and coaching should be provided by the Physical Education teachers. Organisation of these activities starting from planning need to be democratically done by involving pupils in scheduling, planning and organising the sports and games. Inter-class and inter-school competitions and tournaments should be organised to increase efficiency and competitive spirit among the students,. Of course mutual jealousy and ill-feelings are also generated which may be nipped in the bud. There are also the groups and individual activities which should be organised according to the interest and ability of students.

8

School Complex

What is School Complex?

Education is a cooperative process. No stage whether primary or secondary or university is omni-important and can be improved upon keeping itself aloof from others. Isolation is harmful to education as a whole and is a great bar to any kind of educational improvement. This is said to be one of the reasons for deterioration of standards of education at all levels. Persons concerned with university education criticize those at the secondary stage and those in-charge of secondary education put the blame on primary stage. Thus the practice of recrimination prevails the entire educational system and at no stage persons concerned take upon themselves the task of improving the stage, far from cooperatively doing anything in the matter.

Hence many educationists including the Kothari Commission have suggested that in the interest of better education, the spirit of isolation should immediately be replaced by that of co-operation. They have felt that formation of school complex will help in changing this attitude. School Complex is an organised unit in which institutions at the higher stage take upon themselves the responsibility for improving the standard at the lower stage through mutual and voluntary help. The institutions in a school complex, while maintaining their own independence have to realize how their interests are interlinked and how the development of one leads to the development of the other.

How it is organised: According to the Kothari Commission[1] there are about 26,000 secondary schools (at the beginning of the Fourth Plan) and about 14,000 of these in rural areas. In addition, the rural areas have about 65,000 upper primary schools and about 3,60,000 lower primary schools. In other words, in rural areas having a radius of seven to fourteen kilometers there will be about one secondary school, five upper primary schools and twenty-eight lower primary schools. The total number of teachers may be about 80 to 100. This is a fairly small and manageable group which can function in face-to-face relationship within easily accessible distance. It has also a good potential for planning and guidance. There will be at least five or six trained graduates in the group. Moreover, it is possible to provide new aids like a projector, a good library, a good laboratory in each secondary school as a unit and make them functionally available to all the schools in the area. This group built round a secondary school should, in the views of the Commission, be adopted as the minimum viable unit of educational reform and be developed accordingly.

The Kothari Commission have suggested that linking of secondary and primary schools under this scheme can be done in two tiers. In the first tier, each upper primary schools should be integrally related to the eight to ten lower primary schools that exist in its neighbourhood so that they form one "Complex" of educational facilities. The headmaster of the upper primary school should provide an extension service to the lower primary schools in his charge and it will be his responsibility to see that they function properly. For this purpose, there would be a committee under his chairmanship and headmaster of every lower primary school in his area, would be a member. The Committee would be responsible for planning and developing all the schools as a single "Complex". The second tier would be a Committee under the chairmanship of the headmaster of the secondary schools. All head-teachers of upper primary and lower primary schools and teachers can be given a good deal of freedom to develop their own programmes, subject to general guidance of the inspecting staff. It should also be requested to coordinate its work with the local communities and to derive as much help from this source as possible.

1. Ministry of Education, Government of India: The Report of the Education, Commission, 1964-66, (pp. 43-44.)

School complexes in the form of such groups, of educational institutions will be so organised as to be convenient and viable units for making cooperative efforts with a view to promoting standards and securing better coordination between the different stages of education. Instead of isolation, proper articulation can be feasible in these small groups of educational institutions and the situation of mutual recrimination will give place to one of mutual help and fellow feeling.

Advantages — The advantages that would accrue from such an organisation are very obvious. The ultimate objective of the school complex is to promote educational advance mainly qualitatively. As the Commission have observed, it will break the terrible isolation under which each school functions at present. It will enable a small group of schools working in a neighbourhood to make a cooperative efforts to improve standards. The important advantages are as follows:

(1) School complex will offer better human resources for improving the content-knowledge and skills in methodology. As most of the primary school teachers are ill-equipped and under-qualified to do justice to the enriched and improved syllabus and text-books, the experienced and higher qualified teachers of local high schools will help them to make up their deficiencies. Of course for this, free and frank discussion among them without having any complex of inferiority or superiority should be ensured. Any kind of authoritarian attitude on one side and the spirit of "I know everything" on the other will mar everything that is desired from this organisation. The climate of mutual give-and-take will promote the cross-fertilisation of ideas and experience, which is a pre-requisite for any cooperative attempts for improving education.

(2) Due to the limitations of financial or physical resources it is not possible to provide each school with adequate facilities and equipments. But it can be done jointly to all schools in a school complex. Even best laboratory and library facilities can be provided to the nucleus schools. The students and teachers of the complex schools can easily utilize these facilities, namely, for making experiments and conducting practical work in such laboratories and reading and referring

to good books in such well-equipped libraries. The participating schools can also borrow scientific instruments, materials, books and journals from the central schools.

(3) The school complex being a viable unit will enable the participants to try out and introduce better methods of teaching and evaluation. Desirable practices can be disseminated and popularised easily through the educational institutions of a complex.

(4) Instructional materials like scheme of lessons, routines, notes, handouts, etc., can be cooperatively prepared and teaching aids be improvised by the competent and interested teachers of the school complex. Even institutional plans and programmes for school improvement and development can, with profit, be prepared.

(5) School complex will enable the Education Department to decentralise authority and responsibility with comparatively less fear of being misused and provide the necessary stock of talent and resources at the functional level to make use of this freedom and cooperation.

(6) Such organisation can function as a forum of in-service education and as a centre of advancing professional growth of teachers through periodical meetings, conferences, film-shows, demonstration lessons and special courses on various curricular and co-curricular problems.

Functioning of the School Complex

The successful functioning of such organisation largely depends on the interest evinced by the supervisors of the concerned locality as well as by the District/Circle Inspectors of Schools. As visualised by the Kothari Commission they should deal the school complexes as units of small, face to face and cooperative groups. They can safely delegate some of their powers that can efficiently be exercised at local or functional levels. They will frequently be in touch with each school complex and try to make the system more elastic and dynamic. They will provide timely academic leadership and be responsible for effective functioning of school complexes.

The District/Circle Inspectors of Schools have to take the following steps with a view to energising school complexes:

(1) They should organise an orientation course for head-teachers of all schools in the school complexes to explain them the objectives and functions of a school complex.
(2) Subsequently they will provide guidance through on-the-spot visits and correspondence.
(3) They should try to involve the subordinate inspecting officers, Block Development Officers and other local officers in school complex programme in their respective jurisdictions.
(4) They should receive the plans of activities of different school complexes within their jurisdictions and also periodical reports of their working. These will help them to know the kinds of improvement programmes and development projects being implemented through school complexes. Wherever required, they will extend help and encouragement.
(5) They will have to bring about co-ordination between similar projects going on in different schools, so that there will not be any wastage of resource or unnecessary duplication of work.
(6) They will hold or associate themselves with periodical evaluation of various programmes and projects in order to appraise the achievements and shortcomings.

Thus success of the school complex starting from planning to evaluation largely depend on the dynamic leadership, resourcefulness, initiative and personality of the District/Circle Inspector of Schools.

Experiences — Prior to the Kothari Commission certain sporadic attempts were made in different parts of the country for improvement and development of education through mutual cooperation and voluntary help of higher organisations, either in the form of human or material resources. Such organisations had many names and forms. After the Kothari Commission, however, this kind of set-up was known as school complex and became very popular in most of the States. The State Institute of Education, Orissa, also made some pioneering endeavours to improve the content knowledge of primary school teachers with the academic assistance of High School and Secondary Training School teachers. After the introduction of a new syllabus since 1963, it was felt that about 50 per cent of our primary school teachers, who are M.E. passed only, could not do justice to their duties unless some enrichment programmes are taken up for them. Furthermore, most of our primary schools are ill-equipped and as such the teachers could not successfully teach Science and Social Studies in these schools.

As a pilot project, the State Institute of Education, Orissa, therefore started 40 school complexes during those years. The activities of such complexes confined mainly to: (i) clarification of doubts in content areas, and (ii) sharing the aids and equipments by high schools with primary schools. In addition, periodical meetings were also organised by the headmasters of high schools from time to time, where the concerned sub-inspectors of schools and primary school teachers met and demonstration lessons delivered by the high school teachers and academic problems were discussed. Such leading high schools were also given some contingencies for wear and tear of the aid and equipments used and making correspondence work. The progress, however, was not satisfactory so far on account of lethargic attitude and false complacency of primary school teachers on the one hand and indifference and overwork of high school teachers on the other. As local supervising officers, the sub-inspectors of schools have immense responsibilities to motivate primary school teachers and make them need-conscious. The State Education Department had to encourage and energise the existing school complexes and start new ones throughout the State with a considerable amount of financial assistance.

Under NPE, 1986

The National Policy on Education, 1986 and its Programme of Action explicitly mention that an overhaul of the system of planning and management of education heeds to receive high priority. Accordingly to POA (1986, p. 203), "School complexes as a network of institutions on a flexible patterns will be promoted to provide synergic alliance to encourage professionalism among teachers, ensure observance of norms and conduct and enable the sharing of experiences and facilities. The school complex will serve as the lowest viable unit of area planning and will form a cluster of 8-10 institutions in which different institutions can reinforce each other by exchanging resources, personal material, teaching aids etc., and using them as a sharing basis."

It is hoped that in course of time school complexes would take over much of the inspection functions which include inter-alia, educational mapping, grading of institutions and identifying strength and weakness of individual schools. Such inspections will be corrective and not fault-finding in nature and conducted in addition to the normal routine inspection of Inspecting authorities. The State Government should lay down necessary guidelines for qualitative inspections and provide funds for facilitating work of school complexes.

9

Institutional Planning

What is an Institutional Plan?

Education, both qualitative and quantitative, presupposes planning. In a democratic set-up, planning for educational development would provide for participation and involvement at all levels. In educational planning, the participation and involvement of teachers, parents pupils and the public of the locality would promote effective execution and the improvement and development of the educational institutions of the locality can best be facilitated through such local involvement. The educational institutions are the important means of the community for the transmission of culture and the preparation of the younger generation for worthy membership of the community. They have also a claim to the goodwill, resources and endeavours of the community to improve themselves. There should be a plan and programme of action at the institutional level to channelise and utilize them to enable the schools to serve better the purposes for which they have been established.

As Mr. M.B. Buch has succinctly defined, "An institutional plan is a set of programmes prepared by an educational institution on the basis of its felt needs and the knowledge of its resources-available and likely to be available with a view to improving the school standards and practices and with a view to providing for the future development of the institution". The Plan may be for a duration, either longer or shorter, and is based on the principle of optimum utilization of the resources available in the school and the community.

Advantages of Institutional Planning

The main advantage of institutional planning is that it is more realistic. At present we make plans from the top without our firsthand knowledge of the requirements of education in the different areas. Especially our country is as vast as a subcontinent, where planning from the top is a blunder and is also misleading. Without the knowledge of the real needs, such planning is becoming unrealistic and leading to confusion and wastage. That is why, planning at the institutional level is based on realism and real requirements.

As a corollary to this situation, institutional planning is more economical and effective. Of course, every planned work is economical than unplanned one. Since wastage and chaos are reduced to the minimum by proper planning, improvement and development are ensured by it. As such planning is realistic, results stipulated are satisfactorily achieved.

Furthermore, planning done from above, i.e. centre becomes bureaucratic in nature, whereas planning done from below is democratic in spirit as it involves those who are going to be affected by planning. Teachers, students, guardians and local officers are involved in institutional planning. Thus millions of our people will be directly associated with the planning for educational improvement and development and will give the right direction to educational planning in the country reversing the present trend of doing it from the top.

An institution should have a "unique personality" of its own like every individual. With a view to developing it in its own individual line, institutional planning is the best solution and means. On the basis of its individual development there must be its long-term and short-term goals and planning at the institutional level will take them into consideration. Thus institutional planning is goal-based as well as need-based.

Since institutional planning emerges from the "grass roots" involving all—teachers, parents local authorities and even students, it arouses their enthusiasm and releases their energy in realizing the plan targets fixed by themselves. It is, therefore, psychologically much more sound and having more intrinsic motivation. Here the built-in mechanism ensures effective implementation of plans.

Institutional planning provides adequate scope for initiative, creativity, freedom and experimentation, by teachers who are personally involved in the process. It also emphasizes human resources more than physical resources. As such it reduces the expenditure-orientation which our plans have wrongfully acquired through the past years.

Characteristics of an Institutional Plan

According to Mr. M.B. Buch the following are the nature and characteristics of an Institutional Plan.

1. *Need-based* — An institutional plan is prepared keeping in view the needs of the school as felt by the staff of the institution. These needs may be in the area of the school organisation, curricular programmes, co-curricular activities, ancillary services and so on.

2. *Specificity* — Every school has its own image and individuality. The plan for an institution should have its individual lines of development and improvement according to its resources and potentialities. Every institution should, therefore, have its own specific plan.

3. *Optimum utilisation* — The institution plan is not expenditure-oriented. Its major criterion is the maximum utilisation of the human as well as physical resources available in the school and the local community.

4. *Augmenting human efforts* — As a corollary to the maximum utilisation of human resources, there should be deliberate attempts by an institution to augment the human efforts. This is essential for a large number of educational programmes which need imagination, initiative and inspiration rather than finance and physical facilities.

5. *Goal-oriented* — The entire planning at the institutional level is directed towards the national goal, viz., pursuit of excellence in every field. This national goal is the common feature of the plans of all institutions in the country. To achieve this, institutional plans will continuously fix higher and higher goals and thereby the plans will go on continuously improving and developing the institutions.

6. *Cooperative in nature* — The institutional plan is co-operative

venture of all concerned—pupils, teachers and the community. Close involvement of all these agencies is encouraged by this planning process. The head teacher of a school is, however, to play the role of the leader in preparing and organising the plan.

7. *Dual aspects* — Each institutional plan will have two major aspects: (i) improvement, and (ii) development. The improvement aspect will be mainly based on human efforts, whereas the development aspects will require the support and assistance of the community, management and the Government.

8. *Long- and short-term plans* — The plan for an institution will, of course, be of a long-term duration. This duration may be of five years coinciding with the Five-year Plan periods at the State and the national levels. But this does not mean that every project will be for a period of 5 years. Within the broad framework of the five year plan prepared by an institution, there will be a number of projects or programmes extending over shorter duration say, of two years, three years, four years or more.

9. *Reflects the State and the National Educational Policy* — The institutional plan, besides developing in its own "image", will reflect the educational policy adopted at the State and the national levels. Broad guidelines may be issued by the State Education Department for preparation of such plans. The institutional plan will be characterised by following the spirit of the State guidelines, but will have the freedom to add, modify or reject them.

10. *Flexibility* — This is a characteristic feature which differentiates the process of planning from bottom from the one of planning from top. The plans prepared at the State and national levels suffer from the elements of rigidity. On the other hand, institutional plan is highly flexible, always open for modification as demanded by the circumstances. It accommodates all changes, mild or drastic.

11. *Democratic set-up* — Institutional planning implies involvement of all concerned. This is possible only in a democratic set-up, where everybody, high or low, has the worth and dignity. Similarly, planning and execution at the institutional level also promote democratization in the school.

12. *Community support* — Community support through

community involvement is also a pre-requisite of institutional planning. It goes without saying that a good institutional plan will ensure the establishment of a better report with the community.

13. *Improved motivation* — An institutional plan through its successful implementation results into improved motivation on the part of the teachers, pupils, management and community. It will create greater enthusiasm and a sense of be belongingness in all the involved agencies to improve education

Steps in Preparing an Institutional Plan

There are no hard and fast rules for preparing a plan for an institution. No rigid steps are to be followed for the purpose. Because like an individual, one institution differs from another in its background, traditions, size, location, strength, staff, equipments, furniture and so on. Therefore, plan for all institutions cannot be the same or even uniform, rather every institution will have a unique plan of its own for improvement and development. However, some guidelines may be suggested as regards the broad steps to be taken for preparing institutional plans. They are as follows:

1. *Study of the background* — Before preparing a plan for an institution, it is essential to study its background as regards the lines of growth over a period of last five to ten years. The traditions, the extended cooperation of the community, the level of pupils' performance, the rate of teachers' turnover, etc. should be studied. These data through the past years would provide practical guidelines for planning for the future improvement and development of the institution.

2. *Image* — Every institution should have its unique personality. It should have an image of individual features. Accordingly it should have its own philosophy of doing things or own style administration. Such philosophy and image determine certain values, which are ultimate goals for the school to achieve in course of next ten to twenty years. Hence institutional planning should keep those goals in view.

3. *Assessment of needs* — An important prerequisite of planning is the knowledge of needs and awareness of problems faced by an institution. The head teacher, his colleagues, students, management

and the community should sit together and make an assessment of the needs and problems. They have to decide the priorities and areas of improvement also over a period of next few years. This problem census or the need survey of the institution should have two aspects: (i) the improvement needs and (ii) the development and expansion needs.

4. *Survey of resources* — After the assessment of needs and problems, a survey is made of the resources both material as well as human, available in the school and in the community. Sometimes it is found that teachers and management are not conscious of the potentialities of the persons working in an institution. Teachers of a school have different abilities, interests or hobbies and variegated experiences, which should be taken into account while making plans for institutional improvement of the school. This does not cost anything. It only requires resourcefulness and imagination on the part of the school staff.

Similarly, there may be different kinds of teaching aids, which are not utilised by teachers. Existence of these materials is not even known to them all. Hence in the survey of resources available in the school every teacher should be involved closely. It would be better if each teacher concerned with a particular subject will prepare a list of teaching materials and should know how best he could use these aids for improvement of his teaching. Even the school library which is most essential for teachers, is the least utilised facility in a school.

Besides, there are many kinds of physical and human resources available in the local community which could be utilised by the school with profit for improvement of both curricular and co-curricular programmes. For example, among human resources there may be retired teachers, doctors, engineers, postmasters and even farmers and craftsmen who would be glad to render their services for benefit of children, similarly among physical resources there may be dispensary, printing press, farms, small industries, post office, etc. which could be tapped for enrichment of instruction. While planning for an institution all these resources available in the school and in the community will be taken into account.

5. *Planning* — After the survey of resources, steps for planning

should be taken up. In view of the urgency in the subjects or areas as identified by the staff-improvement programmes should be chalked out taking availability of resources into account. All teachers who are interested in planning improvement programmes should be involved in planning the programmes. Different teachers may be entrusted to take up different improvement programmes according to their interest and experiences.

Since a series of projects will constitute an improvement programme, each project should be prepared under the following heads:

(a) Definition of the project

(b) The objectives

(c) Procedures and targets

(d) Educational aids required

(e) Method of evaluation.

6. *Implementation* — This is an important stage, where an improvement plan on paper will be translated into action. There will be a flow-chart or a chain of activities to be performed in course of implementing a project. Here different human and physical resources are to be utilised and activities are to be coordinated. The teachers working on a project should meet periodically and discuss their problems, and progress of the project. All the activities should with certain flexibility under the changing circumstances, follow the steps decided already.

7. *Evaluation* — At this stage an assessment will be made of failures and successes of the project. It should be made at different levels and at different times. Such evaluation may be made by the teachers concerned or by a committee of teachers involved in planning these projects. This is internal evaluation. Some outsiders like the District Inspector of Schools, Sub-Inspector of Schools or any person in the communities interested in the project should be involved in the evaluation. This is external evaluation to be held by a Committee. Lastly, the findings of the Committee along with pupil's opinion and teachers' judgement should be studied together in order to arrive at a

definite conclusion about the success of a project or an improvement programme as a whole.

Experiences

A Seminar on Institutional Planning was organised by the Ministry of Education, Government of India, in collaboration with the National Council of Education Research and Training, New Delhi, in November, 1968. It was held at the Regional College of Education, Bhopal, and provided an opportunity to the participants drawn from Inspecting Officers, Staff-members of Training Colleges and Secondary Schools, coming on deputation from different States to discuss the concepts and methodology of institutional planning. Several experts in the field like Shri J.P. Naik, Adviser, Ministry of Education, Government of India, Dr. B.D. Nag Chaudhuri, Member (Science), Planning Commission, Prof. M.V. Mathur, Director, Asian Institute of Educational Administration and Planning.

Subsequently, a Seminar of District Education Officers of Orissa was held at Bhubaneswar from 25th September to the 30th September, 1969 on Institutional Planning. It was first of its kind in the country and was organised jointly by the Government of Orissa and the Asian Institute of Educational Planning and Administration, New Delhi. The Seminar considered the main problems relating to educational planning and administration in Orissa in general and discussed the State's Fourth Five-Year Plan of general education, patterns and problems of administration and management, planning at the district and institutional levels, community support for school improvement programmes in particular. Many experts and educationists from all over the country also participated in the seminar and presented papers on different problems discussed there.

As decided by this seminar, afterwards the State Institute of Education, Orissa, also took the lead in organising such seminars at different places of the State to popularise and publicise institutional planning. The Asian Institute also arranged for dissemination of information and tested practices in regard to School Improvement, Institutional Planning and related programmes from different parts of the country and outside.

Recommendations of the Kothari Commission on Education Planning

In the light of experiences during the first three Five-Year Plans, the Kothari Commission recommended the following for doing away with the defects in the existing system of educational planning and for evolving out a better one.

The crux of the problem of educational planning in India is to evolve a national policy in education in spite of the fact that education is largely a State subject in the Constitution and that a multiplicity of authorities at different levels make decisions on all aspects of the situation. This is not an easy task and as there is little similar experience to guide us, we will have to evolve our own techniques in most cases. It is also necessary to review and improve our planning techniques.

(a) A review of the first three five-year plans in the different States and at the national level highlights the need to improve the planning techniques in some directions. These have been indicated below:

(1) There has been an overemphasis on achievement of targets in enrolments and expenditure. It is true that expansion was badly needed and expansion will have to continue. But on overemphasis on this aspect leads to neglect of the still more important aspect of quality. Similarly, an overemphasis on expenditure targets tends to distort priorities and often leads to wastage. There is thus a need to take a more comprehensive view of the problem and to evolve a broader pattern of goals, especially those relating to qualitative improvement.

(2) Throughout the first three plans, the general policy has been to do something in every sector or for every programme with the result that the meagre resources available were spread thinly over a very large area. This policy involves considerable wastage. It has, therefore, now become important to concentrate on a few crucial programmes such as improvement of the

quality of teachers, development of agricultural education, provision of good and effective, primary education for all children, liquidation of illiteracy, vocationalization of secondary education, establishment of major universities, expansion and improvement of post-graduate education, increase in the number of scholarships and the development of about ten per cent of institutions at each stage of optimum levels of quality.

(3) The emphasis on reaching expenditure targets to which a reference has been made tends to place a premium on programmes where it is easy to incur expenditure, e.g., construction of buildings or expansion of enrolments. This is unfortunate because there are a number of programmes which call for determined effort, organization, talent and hard work rather than large financial investment. The following are some examples of such programmes:

- Production of literature in the modern Indian languages needed for their adoption as media of education at the university stage;
- Educational research;
- Examination reform;
- Preparation of school text-books and teaching and learning materials;
- In-service education of teachers and officers of the Education Departments;
- Improving techniques of supervision;
- Improving contacts with the local communities and parents;

Providing enrichment programmes and guidance to gifted students and some special assistance to retarded or backward ones.

A number of instances of this type can be cited. What is important to note is that, in the existing situation where the financial resources are limited, it is programmes of this type that need for greater emphasis than those which need heavy financial investment.

(4) Yet another weakness in our planning is the inadequacy of evaluation and research. Since planning is a comparatively new process and we have to evolve our own techniques, it is necessary to evaluate our programme continuously and develop a strong research programme which will enable us to cut down costs and increase the effectiveness of the investment in education, but by and large, this has not been done. Some attempts at such evaluation have been made recently in the Planning Commission viz., the COPP Teams have studied three problems, two of which were not of a major magnitude. What we would recommend is the deep involvement of universities, professional organizations, training colleges, etc., in a periodical evaluation of all major programmes included in the plans and in the development of a large-scale research programme of the lines recommended elsewhere.

(5) The existing machinery for educational planning leaves much to be desired. It is not adequately staffed nor is the personnel engaged in it suitably trained. There is hardly any educational planning done at the district level. The planning cells in the offices of the Directorate of Education are inadequate and staffed mostly by persons who have had no training in the field. Their work also is mostly administrative and financial and confined to the compilation and reporting of educational and financial statistics.

(b) There is need to improve the organization and methods of educational planning and for training competent personnel to staff the planning units in the Central Ministry of Education, the State Department of Education and District School Boards. It should be possible for the Ministry of Education, in collaboration with the Asian Institute of Educational Planning, to undertake studies of educational planning in the different states and to conduct intensive courses for training the personnel involved in the process of educational planning in India. The subject is of such great significance that the UGC should also consider the possibility of setting up an Advanced Centre for Studies in Educational Planning, Administration and Finance.

(c) Education is essentially a responsibility of the State Governments. But it is also a national concern and in certain major sectors, decisions have to be taken at the national level. This implies the need to regard education as a Centre-State partnership. On the other hand, it is necessary to remember that education which concerns every parent and every family has to be taken as close to the people as possible and that its administration can be best conducted by or in close association with local communities. This implies that educational planning has to be decentralized to the district level and still further down to the level of each institution. The process of educational planning in a federal democracy like ours has thus to be the right blend of centralization, in the appropriate sectors, with a large amount of decentralization in other sectors and especially in administration. Care should, however, be taken that the parts fall coherently into the totality of a broad national plan, and all discordant features and contradictions are eliminated. For this purpose, it will be necessary to devise an effective machinery of coordination. This is the direction in which administration has to strive and planning has to grow.

(d) One useful suggestion which can be made in this context is to adopt a system of priorities at different levels—national, state and local. Programmes of national significance such as provision of good and effective primary education to every child, vocationalization of secondary education, post-graduate education and research, or education for agriculture and industry may be regarded as national priorities in the sense that the decisions regarding them would have to be taken by the Centre in consultation with the State and, once they are taken, it should be obligatory on every State to implement them effectively and vigorously. In several other matters, and these would form the bulk of the decisions to be made, a system of State-level priorities should be adopted, i.e., each State may be left to make its own best decision in view of local conditions. These would include problems such as making secondary education free of tuition fees and in such matters, no attempt at a national uniformity need be made. In certain other matters, as for instance, in the provision of amenities in schools, and determining the type and scale of non-teacher costs, a system of local priorities may be adopted. The State Governments may create appropriate authorities at the district and school levels and leave them free to take decisions, within the powers delegated, and best suited to the local conditions. There should be no need to expect any uniformity in these matters between one district and another. A system such as this which centralizes a few essential sectors at the national level would be much better than the present trend to take more and more decisions crucial or otherwise at the national and State levels. This sometimes results in the curbing of local initiative and disregard of local conditions.

10

The Headmaster

Role and Importance

The headmaster plays an important role in an educational institution. He is compared with the captain of a ship. He is also described as the solar orb round whom all the teacher planets revolve. In fact, he is the head of the school both academically and administratively.

The headmaster is the head of the masters or teachers in a particular school. He holds the key position and plans, coordinates and organises various programmes. He ensures proper maintenance of discipline in school. He promotes the harmonious development of the institution. He carries the traditions as well as projects the image of the school according the his own ideas and ideals. It is, therefore, said that a school is as great as its headmaster.

The headmaster should be a man of great head and heart. He must have good qualification in general education as well as in professional training. He must be a person with character and integrity. He should be a learned person and should have faith in himself, in his profession, in his staff and in his pupils. He should inspire all staff, students and public. He should, therefore have adequate proficiency in maintaining proper human relationships with all concerned.

The headmaster is the team leader and the spirit of cooperation should permeate his entire dealings with the staff, pupils and community. He, with close collaboration of his staff, should work for accomplishing the objectives and ideals of the institution set before them. The success and achievements of the school largely depends on his efficiency, ability, alertness, imagination, experience and resourcefulness. In fact, he is the friend, philosopher and guide in school.

Duties, Functions and Responsibilities

The headmaster has a large number of academic, organisational and administrative duties and responsibilities. But for convenience shake, these can be classified into the following:

(a) Planning
(b) Teaching
(c) Organising and Administering
(d) Supervising and guiding
(e) Maintaining discipline and interhuman relations

(a) *Planning*

Planning is the first step in any academic and administrative assignment. The headmaster has to plan all kinds of his activities in time for implementing various programmes with success. He is required to plan his duties and functions throughout the year, but mainly at the following stages: (i) before the opening of the school, (ii) on the opening day and during the first week of the session, (iii) during the session and (iv) at the end of the session.

With a view to planning effectively, the headmaster should involve all including his staff, students, guardians and parents. He has to convene the meetings of staff council, managing committee, parent-teacher association and students council for holding discussions and arriving at the decisions for implementation. Planning should embrace all activities, curricular, co-curricular, projects and community service.

(i) *Planning before the opening of the school* — Unless proper planning is made before opening of the school, there will be a chaotic condition in the school. There may be teachers without students, classes without pupils, classes without accommodation, subjects without teachers and so on, due to lack of timely planning. The headmaster should therefore plan all arrangements before opening of the school so that everything is found ready and as per the needs and conditions. The following tasks need be taken up at this stage:

(a) The headmaster should announce the opening of the session after the summer vacation, the date of application for admission, the date of any admission tests for that purpose and so on. All these may be notified on the Notice Board of the school and/or advertised in the newspapers.

(b) He should make plans for admissions either on the basis of class promotions or holding necessary tests or adopting certain procedures and criteria. This has to be planned according to the prescribed intake capacity, available accommodation and teachers strength.

(c) He should ensure physical verification of all kinds of stock of the school like equipment, furniture, library books and journals etc.

(d) Necessary registers and files should be opened or made up to date according to programmes and projects being or to be undertaken during the session.

(e) A calendar of activities should be prepared for the whole session in advance. It includes, inter-alia, dates for holding admission tests and other examinations, for admission, for applying for fee concessions and so on, school calendar and student diaries can be printed if funds permit and necessary information should be given in these publications.

(f) Steps should be taken for appointment of new staff members due to additional sections/classes, death, and transfer of teachers.

(g) If the school is Govt. managed/aided, necessary proposals should be submitted to Government earlier e.g. for creation of posts, releasing grants/sanctions and so on.

(ii) On the opening day and during the first week of the session planning should be made as regards the following:
   (a) Teacher wise, student-wise and room-wise time-tables should be prepared.
   (b) Individual teachers should develop their scheme of lessons/activities.
   (c) Earlier to this, distribution of work, particularly teaching assignments should be done among the staff.
   (d) Distributions of various co-curricular activities/projects should be made among the teachers.
   (e) Making arrangements for necessary physical facilities like furniture, equipment etc. should be done.
   (f) Students assemblies may be convened to orient the new students and giving necessary instructions.
   (g) Announcements should be made for purchase of text book, notebooks etc.

(iii) *During the session:* The following tasks should be planned by the headmaster throughout the year:
   (a) Organisation of the instructional work.
   (b) Organisation of various projects/co-curricular, activities.
   (c) Organisation of the evaluation/examination.
   (d) Organising extramural talks/extension lectures by experts.
   (e) Organising class-supervision and verification of records, student works etc.
   (f) Organising guidance services, school broadcast programmes and so on.
   (g) Making correspondence, furnishing proposals to Govt. for improving infrastructure and academic programmes.

(iv) *At the end of the session*: The headmaster has to make planning for the following works:
   (a) Holding annual sports, prize distribution ceremonies etc.
   (b) Preparing abstracts of attendance, enrolment, fee collection, expenditure statement etc.

(c) Preparing Annual Reports.
(d) Recording supervision remarks, making class promotion etc.
(e) Taking preliminary steps for the next session.

In this context it may be noted that the headmaster should plan mainly for two kinds of work:

(i) maintenance, and (ii) development. Any headmaster has to manage the school planning and organising some routine activities. But the innovative and resourceful head teacher should make plans for new projects, developmental programmes and improvement of the school programmes and improvement of the school plans.

(b) *Teaching*

The headmaster is the head of teachers. He should be the teacher first and then everything else. He should take some classes, give guidance to teachers and see that teaching work and standard in the school is not impaired in any way. He should command due respect and play a leadership role only by making himself good in teaching and better in knowledge and understanding of the teachers' and students' problems. He, of course, cannot be an expert in all subjects cr fields, but he should have skills, interests and positive attitude towards academic activities.

It is however, found that many headmasters keep themselves so much engaged in administrative and non-academic work that they do not spare time for academic and teaching activities. They thus become the administrative head, not the academic head which is more essential than anything else. They should realize the standards of students and teaching work of teachers, their problems and difficulties, so that they can render necessary guidance for improving the conditions. They should act as the light-house of knowledge and inspiration.

There cannot be any hard and fast principles or criteria regarding the number of periods, higher or lower classes, subjects of teaching and so on to be taken up by the headmaster. It depends on the volume of his administrative and supervising responsibility, his expertise in the subjects, nature of schools and so on. On the whole, the headmaster has to take up some teaching work according to his interest and convenience.

(c) *Organising and Administering*

The headmaster, besides planning, is required to organise and administer various programmes and projects in the schools. At the outset, he must procure adequate furniture; equipment and instruments for the school. He gets the old equipment and furniture repaired, sets up libraries, workshops and other physical facilities in an effective and improved manner.

The headmaster has to develop curricular preparation, classify pupils, distribute teaching jobs among teachers, allotting other duties among the staff through discussion and deliberation. He should organise sports, school broadcasts, festivals, scouting, Red Cross, parent-teacher associations, faculty meetings, staff meetings and so on.

Office work is also an important component of the headmaster's responsibility. He has to make budgeting, correspondences, accounting, verification, checking the up-to-date entries in the registers and documents of the school. Unless he is alert in the matter, there may be forgery, corruption, misappropriation and other difficulties in the administration. Office is the life centre of the school and the headmaster has to maintain it properly.

(d) *Supervising and Guiding*

In traditional sense supervising and guiding are taken as components of administration and organisation. But in the modern days supervision has acquired new significance and needs special skills and insight. Administration, for example means providing physical facilities and ensuring successful functioning of the institution, whereas supervision is concerned with improving the total teaching-learning situation. Modern supervision is not "fault-finding", but encouraging and guiding the teachers and students, even the parents for improving quality of the educational process.

A headmaster should supervise the work of teachers in order to help encourage guide, not to criticise and find faults. He can do this through participation and in a spirit of cooperation. His supervision should be regular and continuous. The headmaster is required to supervise the following work in the school:

(i) *Supervision of the teaching work* — The headmaster should supervise the teaching work done by the teachers regularly and in actual situations. Sometimes he may be required to demonstrate through teaching any difficult point or concept. He should discuss any defects found in teaching of a teacher afterwards in his own office room, not in the classroom in the presence of students. His attitude should be friendly and cooperative. He should instruct by way of guidance.
The headmaster should also supervise the work of students. He may prepare a schedule according to which the monitors will submit the note books of students to the headmasters. He should give his brief remarks regarding the nature and extent of correction and suggestions for improving the situations. The standard and neatness of the student's writing should be evaluated by the headmaster who can give his views for guidance.

(ii) *Supervision of the practical's and out-door work* — Students are required to do map-work, conduct surveys, undertake projects, carry on practical and craftwork in and outside the school. They play games and sports, hold meetings and go on picnics and field trips. The headmaster should supervise these activities every now and then and extend necessary cooperation as well as guidance.

(iii) *Supervision of welfare services* — Provision of adequate physical facilities and welfare for better teaching-learning activities. For example, physical facilities like water and light, seating accommodation and furniture, hostel provision for board and lodging and services like medical inspection, some other facilities like cycle stand, common room, canteen etc. are necessary. All these facilities and services have to be supervised regularly by the headmaster.

(iv) *Supervision of the office work* — As office, as mentioned earlier, is as important as the heart of a body. It has to keep communication both vertical and horizontal. It has to deal with admission, attendance, maintaining registers and accounts etc. The headmaster should supervise all these office work regularly and check up the files and registers from time to time for ensuring proper maintenance and regular drawl as well as disbursement. Otherwise, indifference and callousness on the part of the headmaster will create problems for many, seriously affecting the discipline and morale of the personnel.

(e) *Maintaining Discipline and Interhuman Relations*

Discipline is of vital importance for proper functioning of the school. It depends upon the competency of the headmaster. It is not a particular function or duty of the headmaster. It is an overall outcome of all his activities, dealings and rapport with others. The headmaster has, therefore, to maintain his proper relations with others—staff, students, parents and community.

(a) *Staff* — He must be just and sympathetic towards staff members. He is not an autocrat, but a democratic leader. He should show respect to other's personality and maintain human relationship as congenial as possible. He must recognise the individual differences and capitalise the uniqueness in everybody. He should participate in the actual situation himself and share the burden of work as well as responsibility. He must give instruction and at the same time seek advice and suggestions from teachers both individually as well as jointly. For this purpose, both personal interviews/ discussion as well as staff-teachings are to be held as frequently as possible.

(b) *Students* — The headmaster is not only the leader of the staff, but also a well-wisher of pupils. Through democratic administration he should promote willing participation and sharing of pupils in the management and organisation of both curricular and co-curricular programmes. The headmaster should take keen interest in student's welfare activities and provide all facilities for all-round development of their personality. He should maintain friendly relation with students in order to encourage and inspire them.

(c) *Parents* — The headmaster should maintain both direct and indirect contacts with guardians. It has been found that teachers' close relations with parents and student's achievement as well as behaviour are positively correlated. Parent-teacher association may be formed for the purpose and the headmaster should involve guardians in the annual functions and occasional celebrations in the school. The headmaster should be cooperative, sympathetic and courteous towards them.

(d) *Community* — Since school is regarded as the centre of community development, headmaster should maintain close liaison with the community. There are experts in art, literature, craft, etc., in different sectors of the community and they can be invited to schools to give talks and demonstrate their work to students and teachers. The headmaster should keep contacts with various voluntary agencies and philanthropic organisations to enlist their help and cooperation for promotion of school improvement.

11

The Inspecting Officers

Meaning and Functions

In the modern democratic set up Inspecting Officers are regarded as "Friends, philosophers and guides". Gone are the days when they were regarded as "police" officers whose duties were only to find faults, criticise their activities and punish them. Now they are to encourage, inspire and guide the teachers and students for improving the teaching-learning situations. The inspecting officers are no longer autocrats and authoritarians, but are democrats and benefactors. They are the professional leaders and their expertise as well as experience are banked upon for expansion and improvement of the quality of education.

The Inspecting Officers provide administration and supervision which are concerned with functioning of the educational system at various levels, physical facilities and other services at the schools. They promote innovations and good practices for improving the quality of education. They can make or mark the educational system to the extent and in the manner these officers perform their duties. The Inspecting Officers work at various levels for management, administration and supervision of schools. At the lowest levels of the hierarchy, the Sub-Inspector of schools works for primary schools, then Deputy/District Inspector of schools for lower secondary or elementary (M.E.) schools. At the secondary education level the Inspector of schools function as supervisors and administrators.

All these inspecting officers are required to perform duties of varied and multifarious nature. Their functions can be divided mainly into two types: (i) administrative, and (ii) academic. The administrative duties relate to inspection of schools, sanction of leave, transfers and appointments, issuing circulars and directives from time to time. Their academic duties relate to giving professional guidance to teachers, organising seminars and conferences for discussing curricular and co-curricular programmes, organising in-service training courses for improving the teaching-learning process. Both these functions are, however, inter-related and there is water-tight compartment between them.

1. *The Sub-Inspector of Schools*

The S.I. of schools plays a pivotal role in the expansion and improvement of education, particularly at the primary stage, even though he is at the lowest rung of the educational ladder. His primary duty is in connection with administrative as well as academic aspects of the primary education. The important functions of the S.I. of schools are follows:

(i) *Inspection:* The S.I. of schools is required to inspect the primary schools, pre-primary schools, sevashrams, Chatasalis etc. He may, however, be authorised by the Inspector of schools or District Inspector of schools or Deputy Inspector of schools to visit Middle Schools and Elementary Training Schools. He should also occasionally see the parents and guardians of the pupils of primary schools in order to explain the need for regular and punctual attendance and to persuade the pupils to take interest in education.

(ii) *Tour:* As per the Orissa Education Code, the S.I. of Schools is required to be on tour for more than 200 days annually and to visit and inspect in situ each primary school in his jurisdiction at least twice a year. He must submit his tour programme to the Executive Officer of the Panchayat Samiti (B.D.O.) for approval. The Executive Officer, after approving the tour programme should send same to the D.I. or Deputy Inspector of schools, in case the Dy. Inspector of schools or D.I. of schools suggests any changes in the approved tour programme, he should communicate the same to the

Executive Officer who should see that the changes are incorporated properly. The S.I. of schools should submit with his diary, a full list of the primary, special and indigenous schools in his circle showing the name and nature of each school, the date of its commencement, the date of inspection in various months and any remarks thereon. The form will be returned with the diary. The tour diaries of S.I. of schools are examined by the EDO and his observations are given on the same. Then the same is submitted to the District/Deputy Inspector of Schools.

(iii) *Annual Returns*: Sub-Inspector of schools are required to furnish annual returns in respect to their circles. Then at least one S.I. of schools from each Panchayat Samiti is deputed to the office of the D.I. of schools for preparation of District annual returns at least for ten days inclusive of Sundays and public holidays and days spent on travelling from and to their headquarter.

(iv) *Centre Meetings*: Centre meetings are regarded as the forums of in-service education. These monthly meetings are attended by all primary school teachers. Discussions are held on important educational issues and Government policy matters, circulars and orders are discussed. Demonstration lessons are delivered by experienced as well as newly trained teachers or sometimes by teacher educators of training schools. The S.I. of schools generally preside over such meetings and give his advice and suggestions. Thus the Centre meetings when properly planned and organized serve as an effective means of in-service education, group dynamics and common forum for academic work.

(v) *Annual Conferences*: Although there is no hard and fast rule for organisation of conferences of teachers in one circle or Panchayat Samiti, efficient Sub-Inspectors of schools usually hold such conference annually. All the teachers working in one Panchayat Samiti, efficient Sub-Inspectors of schools usually hold such conference annually. All the teachers working in one Panchayat Samiti assemble for one or two days at a central place and discuss their common academic and administrative problems. Distinguished educationists, educators, leaders and Inspecting Officers address them. On this occasion sports competitions are held, essay competitions are organised and educational exhibitions are set up by teachers.

(vi) *Administrative Duties*: Previously, S.I. of schools was required to appoint and transfer the primary school teachers. Even on his recommendations, District Board and Local Board authorities used to sanction funds for purchase of equipment, stationeries etc. After the Panchayati Raj came into being, the S.I. of schools is regarded as the Education Extension Officers under the Panchayat Samiti or Block Development Authority. He is required to maintain leave accounts, service books, Provident Fund Accounts etc. He also prepares pay bills and disburses monthly emoluments to teachers. Besides, he is even asked to do some non-educational work by the BDO who is his immediate boss. It is, therefore, found that the S.I. of schools fail to do his basic duty—inspection of schools due to lack of time and other engagements. As a matter of fact, quality of primary education instead of improvement suffers from deterioration day by day.

2. *The District Inspectors of Schools*

The District Inspector of Schools popularly known as D.I. of Schools is the District Education Officer in true sense of the term as there was only one D.I. of Schools for the entire revenue district. Subsequently, with a view to facilitating better supervision, more and more posts of D.I. of schools were created and at present, the jurisdiction of a D.I. of schools is mostly delimited to one or two sub-divisions. Thus there are now about four or five D.I. of schools in one revenue district. The D I. of schools is required to perform the following duties:

(i) *Inspection:* He is directly responsible for supervising M.E. and E.T. Schools. He may visit new high schools and secondary training schools with instruction from higher authorities. It is also a part of his duty to visit primary schools, sevashram and pre-primary schools in order to check the work of the S.I. of schools who is his subordinate and also to give a fillip to the development of education in his area. He can also supervise the officers of the Deputy Inspector of Schools and S.I. of schools under his control. He acts as the educational adviser to the District Magistrate or Sub-Divisional Officer.

(ii) *Publicity and Monitoring:* The D.I. of schools should occasionally arrange interviews with the other District Officers to inform and solicit their cooperation in educational expansion and improvement. He should also hold discussion with Managing Committee and guardians as well as parents about the improvement of the schools and various problems faced by schools. He is required to visit and monitor progress of different educational programmes being implemented in his district.

(iii) *Tour:* The D.I. of Schools is required to spend at least 150 days on tour and should inspect each Middle School once a Year and each E.T. school under his charge as often as possible. In addition, he should inspect as many primary and pre-primary schools as he conveniently can.

(iv) *Checking the Work of Subordinates:* The D.I. of schools should check the tour diaries and programmes of S.I. of schools and Deputy Inspector of Schools. He should require each S.I. of schools to submit a full list of the primary, special and indigenous schools in his circle along with his diary. The list should show the name and type of school, the date of its commencement, the dates of inspection in the various months and any remarks thereon. The list should be returned to the S.I. of schools after inspection.

(v) *Annual Conferences:* The D.I. of Schools is required to organise annual conference of S.I. of Schools, Headmasters of M.E. Schools and ET. schools. He presides over the proceedings of the conference, which is held for 2 or 3 days. On this occasion, discussions are made on educational problems/issues and demonstration lessons are delivered on new methods of teaching or on new topic in any subject.

(vi) *Collection of Statistics:* The timely collection of statistics for the annual and other reports in proper form rests with the D.I. of schools. He is to consolidate and compile the annual statistics after thoroughly scrutinising the returns and other data collected by his officers from various agencies and reconciling the discrepancies, strictly according to the instructions issued from the Directorate. He submits the annual statistics of all educational institutions irrespective of control through Circle Inspector of Schools with certificate of correctness and completeness.

Responsibilities of D.I. of Schools

The D.I. of schools is endowed with the following powers and responsibilities:

(1) To countersign the establishment and contingent bills and elementary training schools.
(2) To pass the establishment and contingent bills of Government, M.E. and Middle schools.
(3) To pass bills for Sanskrit stipends, rewards and grants-in-aid to Tols, madrasas and middle schools.
(4) To submit indents for forms and envelops direct to the Superintendent/Director, Government Press.
(5) To sanction the purchase of library and prize books and furniture and teaching appliances manufactured in India up to a limit of Rs. 50/- for each article for Government schools other than High Schools and ET schools.
(6) To sanction the sale of worn out furniture and apparatus belonging to Government schools.
(7) To grant leave, sanction the transfer of pupils and approve the list of holding in respect to all ET schools in his jurisdiction.
(8) To pass bills for M.E. and U.P. scholarships.
(9) To sanction the transfer of U.P. scholarships from ME schools.
(10) To make appointment of menials. There have been some more

duties and responsibilities of the D.J. schools in the emerging trends of educational expansion. Some powers similarly have been found absolute now-a-days.

3. *The Cycle Inspector of Schools*

The Circle Inspector of Schools or C.I. of schools is the senior most officer of the Education Department and his basic responsibility is to see the development of school education, monitoring, visits and advise to the District Magistrate who is the head of the district administration. As per the Orissa Education Code, 1964, the duties and responsibilities of the Inspector of schools (C.I.) are as follows:

1. *Duties of C.I. Towards Govt. Schools*: The Inspector of school is responsible for the efficient inspection of all Government educational institutions in his area excepting Colleges and higher education centres. He is directly responsible for inspection of all recognised high schools in the inspectorate at least once in every calendar year. He is required to send the reports of his inspections to his next higher authority. Each of his reports must contain a definite recommendations as to whether or not the school should continue to be permitted to present candidates at the Matriculation Examination. He should also pay occasional visits to these schools to check their standard and physical as well as academic conditions. Besides, he is required to pay visits to certain percentage of M.E. and primary schools in order to check the work of subordinates.

The C.I. is also required to see that the Department Acts, Rules and Regulations, Government institutions and circulars are strictly followed, the accounts are correctly maintained and discipline is kept in tact in all institutions under his control. He also recommends to the Director about the following physical and personal facilities for improving educational quality:

(i) The construction and extension of the school building, hostels or out-houses.
(ii) Alterations or additions to the staff.
(iii) The provision of additional school material or equipment.

The C.J.'s formal visits to the high schools in his jurisdiction should be undertaken in course of ordinary tours of inspection and should be evenly distributed throughout the year.

2. *Duties Towards Aided Schools:* The Inspector of Schools is the agent of the Education Department and as such administer grants to recognized schools under private management. In course of his inspection to an aided school he is required to see that the conditions attached to the grants are entirely fulfilled, the accounts are correctly kept, departmental regulations strictly followed and discipline properly maintained. He is empowered to recommend the school authorities the dismissal or removal of any teacher with whose work he is dissatisfied or whose presence on the staff he considers detrimental, to make such recommendations with regards to the staff of the school. The provision of suitable buildings, equipment etc. as may seem to him necessary. If the C.I. finds any infringement of the conditions of the grant, or if there is any unwillingness or unwarrantable delay on the part of the school authorities in giving effect to his recommendations, he is empowered to suspend the payment of the grant.

3. *Duties Towards Unaided Schools:* The Inspector of schools has also many duties towards schools getting no grants from Government. Although same efficiency cannot be expected from such schools as it is done in case of Government schools, minimum standard of efficiency has to be ensured in all schools recognised by the Government. If the C.I. considers any school buildings, staff, equipment, or discipline wanting and if the management of the school authorities show unwillingness or unwarrantable delay in carrying out the requirements, he should in case of a high school recommend to the Board of Secondary Education for the withdrawal of recognition and in other cases withdraw recognition for so long a period as he deems necessary.

4. *Responsibility for Examinations:* The Inspector of Schools is responsible for the conduct of departmental examinations and award of middle scholarships in his Inspectorate, in accordance with the Regulations contained in the Code, and subject to the powers exercised by the Board.

5. *Assistance to Revenue Commissioner or District Magistrate:*

The Inspector of Schools is required to furnish to the Revenue Commissioner with whatever information or assistance the latter may require in connection with the work of education in his jurisdiction. In case of disputes between the Management Committee or Advisory Committee of a school and the local people or among the members themselves of these committees, the Inspector of Schools should obtain the opinion of the District Magistrate before giving his decision. The C.I. may reconstitute the Committee, if after consulting the District Magistrate be considers it necessary to do so.

6. *Holding Conferences*: An annual conference should be held in each circle under the presidentship of Inspector of Schools. The headmasters of all high schools and District Inspectors of the Circle should participate in the same. Principals of Training Colleges and other educational experts may be invited to deliver lectures followed by debates and discussions.

7. *Collection of Statistics*: Collection of statistics is of vital importance. The Inspector of Schools is required to collect annual returns and reports from the District Inspectors of Schools and submit the same to the Director in time. It is the duty of the C.I. to get the statistics and statements thoroughly scrutinised at his office in respect of completeness and accuracy, to recollect ail wanting information from the District and other offices concerned.

8. *Delegation of Powers*: Through delegation of powers the Inspector of Schools can make appointments to all lower subordinate educational service and all clerical and menial posts of the Inspectorate, to grant leave of extension of leave, to suspend and impose punishments other than degradation or dismissal in regard to subordinate officers and so on. There are many such financial and administrative powers delegated to the C.I. from time to time. But in the interest of public service these powers are also restricted occasionally.

With a view to enabling the Inspector of Schools to perform his duties properly, steps have been taken to reorganise and strengthen the Inspectorate. For example, in Orissa one post of Administrative Officer has been created in each office of the C.I. in order to share the administrative and financial burden of the Inspector of Schools. It is hoped that C.I. can now devote more time and energy to the academic programmes like supervision, guidance, in-service education and innovation which are badly required for improving the quality of education. Similarly, 13 revenue districts of the State which were formed into 40 Educational Districts have again been divided into 56 for reducing the areas as well as the number of schools under each D.I. of schools for facilitating his work of supervision regularly and comprehensively. The circles of S.I. of schools have also been made smaller in order to minimise their administrative responsibilities. Previously, each Circle of the Inspector of Schools was constituted of two and more revenue districts. But now there are in all 15 circles, each revenue district forming one circle excepting the Cuttack district which has been divided into 3 circles. Unfortunately, in spite of all these reorganizations, the academic programmes have not yet assumed due importance and the administrative duties are putting their heavy load on the Inspector's time and energy.

Truly speaking, the Inspector of Schools should be regarded as the District Education Officer. The Education Commission, 1965-66 has rightly observed, "it is hardly necessary to emphasize the importance of the District Education Officer and his establishment at the district level. He is charged with leadership function in relation to the district as the Director is in relation to the State." (p. 261). The document, Programme of Action for implementation of the National Policy on Education, 1986 has also aptly mentioned, "For ensuring quality of education in educational institutions at different levels, consideration will be given to appointment of District Inspectors of Education to look after academic functions exclusively. Such functionaries who will be selected with due regard to their understanding of the academic functions to be performed, will be responsible for looking after the academic standards in educational institutions provide academic leadership and help in better performance of their academic functions by heads of institutions and teachers" (p. 203). It is hoped that the duties and responsibilities of the Inspector of Schools should be adequately streamlined in the light of the National Policy on Education, 1986 in order to ensure its effective implementation.

12

The Supervisor and His Relationship with Others

Modern Supervisor

Supervisors, in true sense of the term, are democratic, cooperative and creative. They work as educational leaders and guides by virtue of their position, knowledge and skills. They possess special expertise for improving the total teaching-learning process. They are, therefore, professional leaders and inspire as well as motivate the entire group of teachers and students, even the guardians and management to achieve that objective.

The supervisor by virtue of his duties and responsibilities act as a real pivot of the school system. He is not merely to pay visits to schools and issue circulars and instructions to teachers and management authorities. He is rather more interested in preparing and implementing plans for all-round development of the school. The scope of his activities has been broadened and how he has to deal with various functionaries and agencies. They include the school and its staff, the higher authorities on the one hand and the public, the parent and other departmental officers on the other. His relationship with all these personnel should be close, congenial and cooperative. This may be discussed as follows:

1. *The School and its Staff:* The supervisor works in close collaboration with the school for bringing about improvement in the teaching-learning process. He should help the school to work effectively in providing good education. It is his responsibility to

help the staff of the school in improving their professional growth. He should supervise the school regularly with a view to checking its programmes and standard, its development as well as its problems which stand in the way. He practically views the school in the total education system and guides its development in various aspects.

Although the headmaster works as the leader of the group in a particular school, the supervisor acts as the leader of these leaders in a particular district or circle. The headmaster looks into the day-to-day management of the school, whereas the supervisor takes care of the present as well as future educational needs of the entire circle or district under his control.

The headmaster helps his school and its staff to grow whereas the supervisor sees that all headmasters and teachers should develop professionally. The supervisors should possess necessary expertise in guiding them properly and maintain proper inter-human relations adequately. All these will go a long way in the development of education in various spheres.

The headmaster supervises the teaching work of his staff members. He can compare their standard among themselves. But the supervisor by supervising the work and progress of all the teachers in his jurisdiction is in a better position to compare and contrast and give proper guidance and encouragement. The supervisor assesses the performance of the teachers and sets standard for making progress in the right lines. He is in a better position to disseminate good practices and innovations among all the teachers and headmasters. He can inspire and encourage good teachers to do and mediocres to go ahead. Nothing succeeds like success and the supervisor sees that teachers are provided with necessary facilities for improving themselves as well as others including students.

Adequate freedom and flexibility should be allowed in the schools. There should be free flow of ideas and mutual give and take among the schools under the guidance of the supervisor. Close collaboration and cooperation among the supervisor and the school — its staff, headmasters etc., will promote and facilitate the development of education.

2. *Higher Authorities:* The supervisor acts as the liaison officer of the Education Department. He maintains close link between the

higher authorities on the one hand and the teachers, subordinate officers and the community on the other. He has to inform and interpret the policy and orders of the Government to the personnel subordinate to him and report to the higher authorities about their activities and progress made from time to time. Unless he keeps close contact with all these functionaries, he cannot do justice to his job. Rather his reporting may be defective and wrong and he is likely to be misunderstood.

The supervisor has to keep his higher authorities well-informed of the problems and prospects in the field. He reports to them about the programmes and projects being implemented in his area. He should also inform his superior officers about the quality of work performed by his subordinates, the difficulties he and his officers face in discharging their responsibilities, the demands and grievances of his personnel who work with him and under his control.

He should know his duties clearly and act accordingly. He should try to realise his objectives, work proper liasioning, implementing and organising various programmes effectively. He should draw the attention of his higher authorities to such matters which call for immediate action. He should extend all sorts of cooperation to his authorities in their work which is also part of his duties.

3. *The Public and Parents:* The public and parents constitute a major part of the community and schools are established to cater to the needs of the community in educating their children. Most of the schools therefore owe much to the local community for their establishment, improvement, organisation of programmes and management. The public and parents are interested in continuous development of schools. They extend all possible help for improving the standard and activities of schools.

The parents in particular and the public in general desire to be informed about the schools truthfully and continuously. The supervisor tries to take up all possible steps for securing the cooperation of the community for the school improvement. He should try to utilize the school resources for the community and the community resources for the school. But at the same time he should keep the school free from party politics, sectarian conflicts and vested interests.

The public and the parents should be associated with various programmes and projects, functions and festivals of the school which will help them to be acquainted with the activities of the institution. They can contribute to the growth and development of various programmes of the schools. The Parent-Teacher Associations, Guardians Committee, Old Boys Association and Managing Committee should hold their meetings as frequently as possible to discuss the problems and progress of the schools and to help solving problems and accelerate the progress. All these will promote teachers' alertness, students performance, their regular attendance and enrolment.

Modern schools cannot afford to keep themselves aloof from the community. That is why, they are called community-centered. Parents and public have to be involved in various activities and the supervisor should facilitate such interaction, he should meet them as frequently as possible through different occasions. It should be an integral part of his inspection/visit to a particular school, he should invite their suggestion for developing curriculum and sorting out the difficulties for improving the school conditions. Parents and guardians may be invited to discuss some problems like examination results, attendance etc. Exhibition be organised for displaying the children's works, different kinds of literature, drawings and so on. The guardians and parents get pleasure at their son's/daughter's achievement, schemes should take initiative in educating and involving the public. Different co-curricular activities should be organised in the school with supervisors' encouragement. Thus very close cooperation between the Supervisor and the public will facilitate the growth of the school.

4. *Other Departmental Officers:* To bring about development of the School is to enlist the cooperation and collaboration of the inter and intra-departmental officers and personnel. The inter-departmental programmes are dealt with the cooperation of officers of all Departments. Intra-departmental activities are related with various officers of the Education Department. School improvement should be taken as the joint endeavour—and all should extend their assistance in various forms.

The school has assumed the role of a community theatre where all members of the community should participate in different programmes.

The supervisor should invite the officers of various departments to share the developmental activities of the School. For example, for laying down garden and orchard in the School, the help of the agriculture and horticulture officers may be sought. Similarly, for setting up a workshop in the school, assistance of the industry or engineering officers should be useful. With a view to developing diary farming or pisciculture in the school campus for teaching SUPW subjects to students the officers of animal husbandry and fishery may extend their expertise. Thus the Officers of other Departments should be requested to help development of the school curriculum as well as its infrastructure.

The supervisor should be a king-pin for moving the entire school system rightly and adequately. He is to play an innovative and resourceful role for associating officers from various Departments for planning and organising different developmental programmes both in the field of curricular and co-curricular aspects. Besides, academic and intellectual assistance, they can help the school with ample physical facilities that are essential for curriculum development and teaching. The supervisor is thus to act as the catalytic agent of the entire school development. He should spearhead a joint movement of school improvement programme with whole-hearted voluntary support of all inter and intra-departmental officers in the locality.

13

The School-Community Relationship and Managing Committee

School as a Social Institution

The school is a social institution set up for serving specific social needs. It should reflect the life and activities of the society. According to K.G. Saiyidain, "Its (of school) curriculum should be an epitome of their life. Its methods of work must approximate to theirs. It should reflect all that is significant and characteristic in the life of the community in the natural setting". The relation between the school and the community should be close, cordial and cooperative.

Attempts need be made to bring the activities of the school in close touch with the life and activities in the community. These activities should be simplified, purified and balanced in accordance with the abilities of the students. The school is to be regarded as a society in miniature. The knowledge and skills, values and attitudes that are imparted in the school should be related to the life in the community.

School-Community Relation as a Two-way Process

The relation of the school with the community should be a two-way process. The school is established and supported by the community. It also caters to the specific needs of the community. The school should utilize the resources of the community and the community should use the resources of the school.

The community possesses a vast fund of resources like farms. factories, temples, ponds, hills, forests, forts, monuments which are of social, cultural, economic, geographical and aesthetic significance Children should be taken out of the school to explore these resources, so that they can gain new knowledge, widen their outlook, appreciate their heritage and understand their environment.

The members of the community should be united to the school exhibitions, dramatic performances, athletic events, meetings, conferences and other activities, film shows, visits of educationists and national as well as religious leaders, celebration of local, national and international festivals in the school will attract them. Teachers may also be invited to community functions and even to individual family's social as well as religious festivals. They can help the people of the rural community in organising the festivals and other social occasions.

The community can utilise the school resources like school building, school campus, furniture, equipment etc. for organising various programmes. The school can also depend on the community in using its resources, natural, social and cultural for organising the curricular and co-curricular activities of the school. Even the services of village artisans, artists, carpenters, blacksmiths etc., can be utilised for implementing some useful programmes of the school like SUPW.

Mutual Cooperation for Better Relations

All these mutual cooperation and collaboration will promote understanding and appreciation of each other's services and resources. This will strengthen the school-community relation and help improving their rapport for implementing various innovations and organising useful projects which are necessary not only for improving the conditions of the school and community but also developing the all-round personalities.

How to Improve the School-Community Relation

The school should realize that better school-community relation is a pre-requisite for providing good education to children. This can be promoted through the following activities:

The school, particularly teachers should study the needs and conditions of the community. Accordingly, they should organise the curricular and co-curricular programmes of the school. Not only the curriculum should be need-based, but the approaches and methods of implementing the same should be according to the local needs and conditions.

The barrier between the school and community should be removed and communication between them should be promoted by all means. Better the interaction between the school and the community, better is the cooperation between the two.

There should be mutual exchange of resources of the school and the community. The school should utilise the physical facilities and services of the community for improving the curricula and co-curricular programmes. Similarly, the community can utilise the school plant and even the services of the teacher for the benefit of the society.

Some formal agencies and organisations should be developed for facilitating such mutual cooperation and coordination. Some of them are: Parent-Teacher Association, Guardians Meeting, Parents Get-together etc.

The school should not prepare its students only to learn their livelihood or maintain the status quo of the society. It should create productive citizens who can usher in a new society, a new community and a new nation. Adequate social efficiency and constructive mentality of students should be developed by the school through its various programmes.

THE MANAGING COMMITTEE

Evolution of the Managing Committee

With a view to ensuring smooth as well as effective management of educational institutions, there must be democratic and representative bodies with statutory powers and legal status, for the efficient administration. Every educational institution, particularly, private school should have a managing committee for maintaining discipline of the organisation, safeguarding the assets of the school, ensuring standard of teaching and for facilitating the proper service conditions.

The lack of interest of the British Government in expanding education encouraged private managements to establish new schools in various parts of the country. Especially, the introduction of the system of grants-in-aid provided incentive to private managements for setting up a large number of schools extensively and quickly.

Government gradually recognised the Management Committee. With a view to ensuring the standard of teaching and controlling the misappropriation of funds, government framed rules and regulations regarding constitution of the managing committee, rules of business, functioning and powers of these committees/bodies. In fact, they were equipped with sufficient administrative and financial powers to control the activities of the institutions. This included powers of appointment, termination, promotion, suspension etc. even without any prior permission of the Inspector of Schools.

Subsequently, the problems of security of service, discipline etc. arose and agitations were made by teachers against arbitrary and whimsical action of the management. Efforts were then made by Government to regulate the activities of the managing committees, particularly in the privately managed schools. The introduction of the Direct payment system and implementation of the Education Act, 1974 have curtailed the powers, mostly financial, of the managing Committee for avoiding misappropriation, non-payment or delayed payment of teachers' salaries etc.

Managing Committee in Private High Schools

As per Section 7 of the Orissa Education Act, 1969 every private educational institution shall have a Managing Committee or Governing Body as the case may be, constituted in accordance with rules made in that behalf. A Managing Committee or Governing Body, constituted after commencement of this Act in respect of any educational institution shall, before it starts functioning as such, obtain the approval of the prescribed authority i.e., Inspector of Schools. The Managing Committee or the Government Body shall be responsible for the proper management of the institution and shall exercise such powers and functions as may be prescribed.

Constitution of the Managing Committee

The Managing Committee shall consist of not more than 11 nor less than 7 members inclusive of the President and Secretary.

All classes of the community shall be duly represented on the committee. The members shall be of two classes ex-officio and ordinary members. The Headmaster shall be a member of the Committee ex-officio and one of their other members shall be a teacher elected by the members of the Committee shall elect from among themselves a President and Secretary or they may appoint one of the ex-officio President or Secretary during his period of membership.

An ex-officio member of the Managing Committee other than the headmaster and any ordinary member may be removed from office by a resolution to that effect passed at a meeting specially called to consider the question provided that the resolution is supported by the votes of at least three-fourths of the members present and voting. All appointments, resignation or removal of the members of the Committee shall be at once reported by the Secretary to the Inspecting Officer in-charge of the school. The Secretary shall obtain new member's written acceptance. The term of office of ordinary members shall not exceed three years and one third of ordinary shall vacate office every year and to secure this sufficient number of those who have held office for less than three years and more than one year shall be balloted out. Any member failing to attend four consecutive meetings shall cease to be a member and Secretary shall report the matter to the concerned Inspector of Schools. The Committee shall annually appoint an auditor who shall examine the school accounts etc.

Rules of Business

(i) In all matters relating to school building, appointment, punishment and dismissal of teachers and other questions relating to school, the decision of the Committee is final.

(ii) An ordinary meeting of the Committee shall be convened by the Secretary once every month and a special meeting shall be called by him when a requisition of such a meeting is made by not less than half the members of the Committee.

An emergent meeting may be held when necessary with twenty four hour notice. A resolution passed at a special or emergent meeting however shall be subject to confirmation at the next ordinary meeting.

(iii) All meetings shall be held in the school premises.

(iv) The notice of each meeting shall indicate the business to be transacted at the meeting and no other business shall be transcended, except with the consent of three fourths of the members present.

(v) Four members shall form the quorum.

(vi) In absence of the President one of the members present shall be elected to preside and the President shall have a casting vote in addition to his ordinary vote, when the votes are equally divided.

(vii) The Secretary shall keep a record of the proceedings, of each meeting and shall carry on correspondence with proper authorities on behalf of the Committee.

(viii) He shall make all payments except for the allotment which the headmaster is authorised to spend.

(ix) He shall exercise the power of granting leave to teachers.

The Education Act, 1974 has imposed certain restrictions on the powers of the Committee. The introduction of direct payment system has very much affected the financial powers of the management. Under the provisions of the Education Act no educational institution shall receive any aid or grant from the State Govt. if the Managing Committee acts in contravention of the provisions of the Act. Restrictions have been imposed on the Managing Committee's powers to terminate the services of the teachers without obtaining a prior approval in writing of the concerned Inspector of Schools. The Managing Committee cannot close down an institution without intimation to the State Government its intention to do so at least 12 months before the proposed date of closing down the school.

Managing Committee of the Government High School

Constitution: Every Government High school should have a Managing

Committee consisting of the District Magistrate as President, the Headmaster as Secretary, a representative of the teaching staff, the District Inspector of Schools and three non-officials to be appointed by Government and to hold office for a term of three years. The Inspector of Schools is authorised to attend meeting of the Committee at which he considers his presence desirable and to give his opinion on the matters under discussion.

Rules of Business: The Managing Committee must meet at least twice a year, but ordinary transaction may be disposed of by circulating the papers. The Committee has powers to make appointments to sanctioned posts of Superintendent and Asst. Superintendent of the hostel. It has power to appoint the librarian and menial servants.

The Managing Committee should be given freedom as well as responsibility for performing its duties properly in democratic set up.

Summary and Concluding Remarks

The school is an age-old formal institution of education. Its role and functions have undergone changes through ages. The modern school not only gives knowledge and skills, but also trains the future citizens of the country.

The school is a social institution catering to some specific needs. It should maintain good relation with the community. But the school-community relation is a two-way process. The school should provide education according to the needs and conditions of the society. It should make its resources available to the community programmes. Similarly, the physical as well as human resources should be utilised for organising school programmes. Various steps should be taken for improving the school-community relation which is necessary for ensuring good education.

Managing Committee is essential for smooth functioning of the school. It plays an important part in safeguarding the school assets, ensuring standard of teaching and maintaining discipline. It enjoys some statutory powers and a legal status. But the latest Education Code, 1969, and the Education Act, 1974 have imposed some restrictions on its powers and functions for controlling the arbitrary action.

There are some differences in the constitution, rules of business, powers and functions of the Managing Committee of the Government and Private High School. In a democracy like ours the Managing Committee should be given freedom as well as responsibility for properly performing its duties.

14

Teacher-Parents Association and Voluntary Organisations

Need and Importance of Parent-Teacher Cooperation

It has been discussed in the earlier chapter that school-community relation should be close and cordial for ensuring quality in education. This relation is also a two-way traffic. The school should participate in the community programmes and utilise its resources for improving its programmes both curricular and co-curricular. Similarly, the community should share in the school programmes and utilise its services and facilities for development.

On behalf of the school, teachers should take initiative in this process of interaction and cooperation. On behalf of the community, parents should respond and reciprocate warmly and effectively. Both should collaborate in the process in their own interest, in the interest of the school, in the interest of education and in the interest of the community. This exchange is in the mutual interest of all concerned.

Parent-Teacher Association as a Formal Organisation

Parent-Teacher Association is an effective formal organisation for facilitating this school-community collaboration and interaction. It should be formed in every school for the purpose of exchanging ideas that will help them in understanding each other's point of view and that also help in the common task of giving a better, more rational, more healthy and more sympathetic deal to children.

It has been rightly observed by George Tomlinson, "In particular, remember that any clash between parents and teachers must always be harmful to the child. Harmonious working together can alone bring us the results we want." Pupil's welfare is the sole and common objective of both parents and teachers. This is the common goal for which both should try. It can be achieved if both can cooperate and it cannot be achieved if they fail to do the same. Both parents and teachers are custodians of children's development, physical, mental, emotional and moral. Unless they join their hands most cordially, the common goal cannot be reached and it will elude the grasp.

Parents should extend necessary cooperation to teachers for a better and fuller understanding of the child, for sorting out problems that are faced in providing good education to children. Adequate funds should be made available to teachers for providing necessary physical facilities in the schools. For improving academic programmes also parents should furnish the relevant data to teachers. There are individual difference among pupils and adverse situations at homes which have great impact on the teaching-learning process.

But teachers should establish proper rapport with the parents who can develop regard and confidence in teachers and provide all kinds of information for the pupils' well-being. A favourable disposition towards each other will reduce the pupil's way-wardness, negligence in study and lapses in dealings.

Constitution of PTA and its Programmes

Parent-Teacher Association should be formed in each and every school. It will be chief instrument of bringing the school and home closer to each other. It will be a voluntary organisation and any kind of imposition of restriction will harm rather help the purpose. All teachers and parents will automatically be the members of the Association. Since it is a democratic organisation, the office-bearers including the President and Secretary should be elected by the parents and teachers.

The PTA Should sit at least twice or thrice a year and the progress, problems and programmes of the pupils should constitute the main agenda for discussion. The proceedings should be properly maintained and all should be encouraged to participate in the proceeding. Any person or persons or a particular group should not be ailowed to predominate the proceedings. Everybody should express his ideas, feelings and opinions about these matters frankly and openly. No politics, religion or language should have upper hand or superiority in these discussions and decisions.

Parents and teachers should try to help each other through this organisation in solving the pupils problems, may be common to both. Teachers' work should be recognised and their status be given due importance, so that they would feel honoured and happy about their position. Similarly, the parents should be given due regard and a feeling that the school is theirs and it has to be properly maintained and improved in their own interest – well-being of their children.

The PTA in its meetings should discuss the academic problems, but too much of them will be boring and majority of the members cannot participate in the discussion. Rather administrative and supervisory problems which have bearing on the academic ones like performance of students, their attendance, supply of text books, procuring equipment and audio-visual aids, should be discussed and solutions be found out in an objective manner. The PTA may appoint a sub-committee to go into some problems of crucial importance and suggest measures for improving the situations with fact-finding data.

Some important functions of local and national importance may be organised by PTA. For examples, Teachers Day may be organised by the parents-members and Parents Day may be celebrated by teachers of the PTA respectively. With cooperation of parents, the celebration of Saraswati Puja, Ganesh Puja and national festivals etc. will be successful. Organising exhibitions, sports competitions etc., in the school would be more effective and meaningful with cooperation of PTA.

PTA will provide an effective forum for exchange of ideas, experience and opinions on burning issues and problems of the school. It will give a representative sample of cross section of the people—teachers, parents, guardians, of various socio-economic position and conditions. The decisions taken here can be more authentic, judicious and meaningful. The reports on various programmes of the school and success stories of teachers and students will provide new insight, inspiration and enlightenment. Thus the PTA will act as a democratic body giving new directive and drive for further development of the school.

Voluntary Organisations Through Ages

In the ancient India almost all of the educational institutions were of private origin. The private initiative was mostly taken by the landlords, or by philanthropists or by religious organisations. Subsequently, the kings or rulers of the land took interest in establishing educational institutions. The Ashramas of the old Rishis, Vihars of the Buddhists, village chatasalis of the medieval period and Maktabs and Madrasas of Mohammedans period were mainly due to private enterprise.

The East India Company in the beginning did not assume any responsibility of education. During that period voluntary or private institutions of education owned by Hindus and Muslims continued to thrive and contribute their mite to the field of education. The Christian Missionaries also opened a large number of school in various parts of the country and immensely helped the expansion of education.

Since 1813, however, the East India Company started giving grants for the educational programmes of the voluntary organisations. In 1835 the British Government sanctioned a big amount of grants for propagation of English education as per their new policy. The Wood's Despatch of 1858 encouraged the opening of more private schools with Government support. The grant-in-aid scheme, however, benefited the Missionaries most.

The Hunter Commission of 1882 recommended against opening Government schools and suggested that private institutions should be given liberal grants. Thus the private and voluntary organisations got prominence in the field of education. The system of grant-in-aid continued for a long time. Some restrictions were gradually imposed on private agencies to check the growth of poor standard schools and its related evils.

After Independence the policy of encouraging private participation on the provision of education continued without much changes. More and more restrictions were imposed on voluntary agencies in the public interest. Private agencies thus have been playing an important role in the development of education in this country. Many voluntary organisations have earned great distinctions and reputation for their outstanding contribution in the arena of education.

Pros and Cons of Voluntary Organisations

The advantages in the growth of Voluntary Organisations are as follows:

(i) It is a Constitutional right of the citizens of the country to get and provide education according to their sweet desire. Under the Article 30 (i) of the Constitution of India the minority groups whether based on religion or language have been given the Fundamental Right to set up and administer educational institutions of their choice.

(ii) The voluntary organisation take initiative and explore possibilities in the new field. For example, the organisations like Missionaries set up schools in the hilly, wild and backward areas for expanding Primary and Secondary Education. At present many voluntary organisations have done spectacular work in the field of pre-school or early childhood education which is a felt need of the time.

(iii) In a democratic state, the parents have the right to choose the school for their child. Although the Voluntary Organisations charge higher tuition fee, many parents prefer to spend the amount for ensuring better education for their children.

(iv) Although it is complained that existence of private schools encourages class distinction, this is not true. Rather it is mainly due to economic inequalities existing in the society. Abolition of voluntary institutions will not do away with class divisions.

(v) In maintaining voluntary initiative and participation in education, the public treasury is saved of the expenditure which the parents contribute in the shape of tuition fees and donations.

The disadvantages as pointed out by critics of the voluntary/ private organisations are the following:

(i) The voluntary and private organisations perpetuate class distinctions. Because rich people provide better education for their children in expensive school where as poor people are left with poor education in ill-equipped schools.

(ii) The wealthy and influential people are satisfied with good education available for their children in private schools without raising any voice or taking any steps for improving the quality of education.

(iii) Most of the private and voluntary organisations are set up and managed on commercial basis. Adequate and good staff members are not appointed and suitable physical facilities are not procured for good education. Other harmful effects are also experienced on account of managing schools with profit motive.

(iv) Many voluntary schools are denominational which encourage narrow religious and fanatic practices. All these are very detrimental to the very spirit of secularism and national integration.

It may be concluded that with adequate supervision and evaluation, proper standards can be maintained and spirit or national integration as well as secularism can be promoted in the private organisations. In democracy every citizen must be allowed to enjoy his constitutional rights including Right to Education. Unless Private and voluntary organisations share the burden of expenditure on education, it would be difficult on the part of the state to bear the entire responsibility. There should also be reasonable restrictions on payment of salaries to teachers, collection of capitation fees, teaching of religious education etc. so that instead of creating any problems, voluntary organisations can help in accelerating the progress of education in the country.

Views of Commissions and Committees

According to the Education Commission, 1964-66, the activities of the Private and Voluntary Organisations should be governed by the following guidelines:

(i) Since the private agencies have played an important part in the development of education in the modern India and many good institutions are in the private sector, it is hoped that private organisations can continue to make a useful contribution to the development of education in the years ahead. The state should, therefore, make all possible use of the assistance that can come from the private sectors for development of education.

(ii) The growing educational needs of our country should be met by the Government and it would be wrong to expect too much from private sector. The voluntary organisations can only play a limited role.

(iii) Under the Constitution, private schools have a right to exist and if these do not seek financial assistance or recognition from the State, there need not be any considerable restrictions on their activities.

(iv) The private educational institutions which depend very largely on public revenues for their existence, should be gradually assimilated with the system of public education.

(v) Reasonable system of grant-in-aid and control should be adopted for private schools. Desirable safeguards are to be taken regarding economic, social and professional status and security in service conditions of teachers working in voluntary organisations.

The National Policy on Education, 1986 has clearly mentioned that an overhaul of the system of planning and management of education will receive high priority. The NPE inter alia, has stated, "giving pre-eminence to people's involvement including association of non-governmental agencies and voluntary effort as an important guiding consideration for the purpose (p. 8).

The private and voluntary organisations have to play a very significant role in the successful implementation of the programmes like adult education, non-formal education, early childhood education, education of the disabled etc. It has been suggested in the POA that government should take positive steps to promote their wider involvement of voluntary organisations. Hence adequate logistics should be developed for frequent consultations between Govt. and voluntary agencies. The voluntary organisations should be assured necessary facilities to participate in implementation of programmes and procedures for selection of voluntary agencies and of financial assistance will be streamlined to enable the voluntary agencies to play optimal roles. (p. 204)

Summary or Concluding Remarks

Parent-Teacher cooperation is essential for ensuring quality in education. Parent-Teacher Association is a formal organisation for facilitating such cooperation and interaction. PTA should be formed in every school as an instrument of bringing the school closer to the home. It will be a voluntary organisation and all teachers and parents will be its members automatically.

Parents and teachers should try to help each other through PTA in solving the pupil's problems. Proper rapport and understanding should be developed among parents and teachers to make PTA effective. Pupils' welfare is the sole and common objective of the parents and teachers and it can be achieved by the PTA most successfully. The programmes of the PTA can be organised accordingly. It will be a potential forum for exchange of ideas, experience and opinions on burning issues and problems of the school.

In the past private and voluntary organisations played an important role in the development of education. After Independence also, private participation in the expansion of education has been encouraged with some restrictions being imposed in the public interest. There are both merits and limitations of the voluntary organisations. But with adequate supervision and guidance, proper standards can be maintained and judicious sharing can be encouraged in the expansion as well as quality improvement of education.

The Education Commission, 1964-66 suggested that voluntary organisations should be encouraged to participate and contribute to education with reasonable grant-in-aid system and desirable safeguards. The National Policy on Education, 1986 has also said that pre-eminence should be given to people's involvement including association of non-government agencies and voluntary organisations. Especially, voluntary agencies have to play a significant role in the field of adult education, non-formal education, pre-school or early childhood education.

15

School Organisation—School Plant and Building

Meaning of School Organisation

> "To Organise" as per dictionary, means to arrange and form an organic whole; and to coordinate and prepare for activity. So Organisation is the combination of necessary human efforts and material equipment brought together in systematic and effective correlation to accomplish the desired results. W.M. Ryburn; however, writes, "Organisation is not primarily a matter of arrangements, time-tables, schemes of study, types of building, registers and curricula. It is primarily a matter of our attitude to our work and to those with whom we work. The aim of our work and the children with whom we work are our first consideration".

In education, organisation deals with educational practices. It is more than a frame or a chart of work. It is said as the dynamic side of educational process and is indeed the process of management of educational affairs. Educational administration is management of educational affairs. It deals with educational institutions right from the Schools to the Secretariat and it is concerned with both human as well as material equipments. The human elements include children, parents-teachers and other employees in general at local, State and National levels of Government. On the material side come money, buildings and site, teaching equipment and instructional supplies. An integration of both these components goes in the name of educational administration.

Graham Balfour writes very aptly, "purpose of educational administration is to enable the right pupils to receive the right education from the right teachers at a cost within the means of the State which will enable pupils to profit by their learning". In education, school is an organisation of cooperation and as such, it forms a Cooperative Society. Generally, the school organisation emphasises cooperation between headmaster and staff, between headmaster and pupil, between teachers and pupils and between school and parents.

Planned organisation of these physical resources or material equipment in the school is known as "School Plant". Material Equipment is to the school as machinery to the Factory and as tools to the workman. Can a workman work any tool? While it is proverbially true that bad workman blames his tools; it is certain that the best work can only be accomplished with the best tools. So Planning and Management of School Plant is one of the important responsibilities or the headmaster of schools. And so, the school plant equipment and management of these facilities are of tremendous importance in education.

An Evolution of School Plant

Education was not compulsory in the days of old, except Sudras, practically everybody had the opportunity to receive education. Schooling in ancient India was not divorced from life and community. Guru Ashrams served as Schools and were situated far away from towns in the natural surroundings of greenery and foliage. The question of providing special building for schools at large casts, did not arise then. A thatched cottage was enough. Later on schools were housed in temples.

Also in ancient Greece education was given in temples; in ancient Rome, education was being imparted in closed space or verandah adjacent to streets. During middle ages in Europe, the Church took responsibility of schools and those found their shelter in the Churchyard. In Buddhist days, Maths were erected and for higher learning grand buildings were constructed to house Universities like Nalanda, Takshasila and others. Muslim education was provided in Maktabs and in Mosques. Separate houses for schools were hired in

India only after the 16th century. Even in the 19th century, schools in Europe and in England were housed in dark and dingy quarters with low sanitation and bad ventilation.

During the British regime in India, after Wood's Despatch (1854) the Government took the responsibility of opening schools. Some schools were opened here and there mostly in the urban areas and a modest beginning was adopted in equipping schools materially on the western pattern.

The 20th century world found much material advancement in School Plant due to advancement of Science and Technology. Almost everywhere conditions changed rapidly and better School buildings were provided.

But India still remained backward. Even how, majority of elementary schools function almost in open air. Most of the Secondary Schools do not have adequate accommodation and equipment sufficient for the growing number in India's Five Year Plans. With high population pressure, with rapid expansion of education, with continuous increase in enrolments, with the diversification of courses and with an overall demand of better schooling conditions, it is imperative to plan a new material equipment for each elementary and secondary school. Poverty and lack of material resources may stand in the way of right type of planning for the same.

School Plant

The school is a social institution, set up by the community to serve its ends. The physical facilities as well as the school campus contribute a great deal to the total success of school. Learning environment plays an important role in the whole learning process in schools. So the importance of school environment is very clear, since pupils spend a good deal of their time in the school premise. Beautiful surrounding is a very important factor in generating a congenial atmosphere for work. Certainly a first rate campus, building and other facilities create a sense of pride both in the pupils and the members of the staff in the school. Non-functional, meagrely equipped and unattractively decorated school plants have got a poor effect on the children and their teacher.

Now in these days of advancement of Science and Technology, school plants have come up with comfortable seating arrangements, attractive decoration, superior lighting, useful service facilities, such as library, play ground, class rooms with chalk and bulletin boards, toilets with sinks, pupils lockers etc. And due to financial handicaps all these requirements may not be met by all schools. It is a fact that even the most efficient headmaster and the choicest of the staff will remain handicapped for want of proper material equipment.

It is really regrettable to see young children who are huddled together in dark and dingy rooms and made to sit on verandah on unmatted floor or under scanty shade or trees in the scorching heat of summer or in an old and forbidden building adjacent to a dark and narrow lane in a thickly peopled city. Even now there are schools in India without minimum facilities like black board, furniture, play-ground, and library.

Any available place may not be suitable for schools. Whatever may be the type of schools, certain important requirements have got to be fulfilled. Mudaliar Commission (1952-53) has opined that the selection of a site will mostly depend on, weather the school is meant for the rural or urban area. Rural schools should be established in villages with a good number of population, which are easily accessible to the surrounding villages and there should be enough of open space for playgrounds and co-curricular activities of the schools. With a view to diminishing pressure on urban schools, the Commission recommended the establishment of residential rural schools, as there is difficulty in selecting sites for urban schools.

The India Education Commission (1964-66) recommended that in view of the present unsatisfactory position regarding school building, it is required to clear the backlog of unobstructed school buildings. Also it is necessary to provide additional buildings for new enrolment. And as such, allocations should be increased in the Central and State budgets. Loans and grants-in-aid should be given on a liberal basis to private schools for construction of buildings. Due to the shortage of traditional building materials, well designed kacha structures should be accepted as part of the school system. Economy in construction of school buildings should be effected by using locally available materials. To avoid delays in construction of Government buildings, a separate unit of PWD should be set up for the execution of educational building programmes.

The details about school buildings will be given separately. The following may be taken into consideration while making site selection for the schools:

1. A good location should be the deciding factor. The low cost schools will not be always the prime consideration. Thus the cheapest site in the long run may prove otherwise more expensive.
2. The school building should be established outside the town area. As far as possible, it should be kept free from the din a bustle of town life. The heavy traffic routes should be avoided to minimise the danger to children, on their way to school.
3. The schools should be given places where there are much space. Above all, the child requires space to be active.
4. The site of the school should be in the centre of the school population to be served. As per the standing national norms, the elementary school children should approach schools walking a distance of 1 km. and secondary schools pupils, not more than 3 kms.
5. The site should have pleasing surrounding which gives children a comfortable stay in the schools.
6. The school site should be a little raised in level and at any rate it should be dry. There should not be low land with standing water very near to the school.
7. The proposed school site should have direct play of sun light for quite a good part of the day.
8. Care should be taken to avoid low lands subject to flood.
9. The site should permit gardening and agriculture farm.
10. The site should provide sufficient space for future expansion of the school plant.

Class Room

There should be as many class rooms as there are sections in different class in the secondary schools. Each class room should accommodate

40 to 50 pupils. It is desirable that some rooms should be designed to seat about 80-90 students in case of correlated and combined teaching of two sections in one period. Each class room should have essential equipment of desk and chairs for the pupils, wall black-board and a black-board resting on a stand, a chair and a table for the teachers and a map stand. Besides, a dias or a raised, platform for teacher's use, an almirah or cup-board carved into the wall for books, attendance register, chalks, duster, ceiling fan and wooden rail round the room with hooks and nails for display of charts should be there in each class room. Bulletin board, water basin, dust-bin, doormat, table cloth, flower-pots curtains etc. may be among non-essential equipment to decorate the class room. The walls of class rooms should be painted with some light colour. The size of the class room should be 600 sq. ft. (30 × 20) and the height should not exceed 15'.

School Hall

The school hall is an important general-use facility in the Secondary School Plant. Here all the pupils assemble for general meetings, dramatics, lectures, exhibition and many other school activities for the entire student mass. The hall should be located on the ground floor ensuring easy access to the pupils, teachers and the public. The hall should not be less than 2000 sq. ft. The speaker should be audible in every part without any strain on either side, the speaker and the listener. The school hall can be used as multipurpose room as an auditorium, gymnasium, refreshment room, the audio-visual room. Also this can be used on certain special occasions to accommodate parents, teachers and students. There should be adequate arrangements for light and proper ventilation.

Special Rooms

Classrooms are meant for teaching subjects of general nature. Besides the school plant should have accommodation for teaching of some specific subjects like Science, Mathematics, Geography, History, Drawing, Crafts, Music, Home Science etc. The need for special rooms is increasingly recognised for specialised teaching in the subjects due to the impart of modern educational theories. This creates an atmosphere of the subjects for the pupils. The special rooms help economising time and energy, when the equipment, apparatus and other teaching aids are not moved from one end of school to another. It is more risky to move breakable items. Even a durable object like globe may be subject to breakage and defacement, when moved from one classroom to other, almost daily. So, the school plant at the secondary stage and at higher secondary stage (+2) should be provided with special rooms for special subjects.

Science Laboratories

Every Secondary and Higher Secondary School must possess well-planned and well-equipped Science rooms and Laboratories. The old practice of having separate lecture and practical rooms is how giving place to multiple-use room. The size of such room should be 24' × 42' in an average. The service connections for gas, electricity and water are to be provided in the wall of the multiple-use room. This arrangement will facilitate to use movable tables in one position for class work and in another for laboratory. Built-in cup-boards for storing chemicals and apparatus should be provided to each student. This process will go to save much space and the Laboratories will provide a better look.

Library Room

The modern techniques of teaching demand that the library should be the centre of the school educational programme. It is the most important facility in the school and it improves academic life of a school. The library hall with reading rooms should be of 24' × 80' size. The Secondary School Library should be located so as to make it easily accessible to all. The library should have an adequate collection of books, magazines, journals giving most up-to-date and advanced information on all school subjects.

The School Office

Office room should be centrally located to serve as a good

coordinating centre for the school. It should be easily accessible to all concerned, the visitors, the teachers, the pupils and the general public. The school office in a large secondary or higher secondary school should possess a room for the headmaster, a waiting room for visitors, an office room for clerks and a store room with shelves and wall cup-boards for office files. For an efficient functioning, the school office should have modern equipment like Type-writer, Duplicating machine, Desk calendar and Rubber stamps. A fire-proof vault or safe must be there in every school office for the safe keeping of cash and confidential records.

Staff Room

A room can be made available to teachers where they can meet each other. From here they may work together or individually. This may be a waiting place for teachers in between working periods. This room should have cup-boards in the wall or lockers may be there, where the teachers may keep their class written works, examination papers and other things safe.

Workshops and Sheds

Under the new pattern (10+2) of school system, vocationalization of education has found a prominent place in the school curricula. A number of vocations like Carpentry, Smithy, Metal fittings, Electrical works, Repair of household gadgets, transistors-assembling, repair or automobiles etc. have been introduced. In the Higher Secondary Schools, a number of groups as Agricultural Group, Mechanical Group, Civil Engineering, Textile Engineering etc. have been provided. All these necessitate well-equipped workshops and sheds. Specially these should be located on the ground floor.

The School Hostel

Of course with the rapid expansion of schools the need for hostel is decreasing. Yet it is an important institution, where pupils learn punctuality, discipline, citizenship, regularity in work and leadership habits. The hostel should be in the school campus and must be housed in a proper building with good sanitary arrangements. The school hostel should be a single storeyed building, quadrangular in shape and with a courtyard at the centre. On three sides dormitories for pupils can be constructed. The fourth side should contain kitchen and dining space. At the back of this kitchen wing, bathrooms may be located. Latrines and urinals may be provided at little distance from the main hostel building. One of the members of the teaching staff should be selected as Superintendent of the school hostel. His quarter should be located at a little distance from the main gate of the hostel.

Teachers' Quarters

These are considered as an integral part of the school plant. Such quarters will enable to stay in the village, in their place of work. This will assist in improving the standard of instructions in the schools. For the women teachers, the quarters must be provided in the school. The Secondary Education Commission Report says, "we feel that the presence of the headmaster and the staff in or near school, particularly if there are hostels attached or where the schools are residential will be of the greatest benefit to the school-going population. A minimum three-roomed quarters with open space should be provided to every teacher on the campus".

Besides, the school plant should be provided with storage rooms, school farm and agricultural shop, the school playground, art room, music room, medical examination room, school canteen, museum and above all, office for the school counsellor and the career master in the school campus or very near the campus.

School Bidding

It is said that "Buildings are to education as body is to the mind". As a sound mind can only be there in a sound body, so fine buildings make a fine school, and similarly, a poor building, a poor one.

The school is a social institution, set up by society to serve its ends. Beautiful surroundings is a very important factor in generating a pleasing atmosphere for work. So the need for school buildings in

India at different levels of education is tremendous. This is evident from the following calculation. The Working Group on General Education for the Fourth Five Year Plan calculated that Indian School System is in short of nearly 53 crore sq. ft. space. 50 per cent of the Elementary Schools in India are in rented or in extremely unsatisfactory buildings. At only Rs. 10/- per sq. ft., which is the modest sum, the cost of clearing the backlog of unobstructed or half-constructed buildings would be Rs. 530 crores. So the enormity of the problems of school buildings in India is evident.

Really the task for providing 'Schools for all', is a stupendous task. India's resources is limited, it is a call before the planners and administrators in the country, that every rupee to be spent is to be fully utilised to the least paise. If the school buildings are put in manner and design as in the past, it will not leave India with enough resources to undertake improvement in the quality of education in the status of teachers or provision of equipment and other necessary material needs of the school. So in the present position in India, the question arises, what needs to be done with problem of providing for our schools.

Planning and Designing School Building for Elementary Schools

In the Independent India during the last Five Year Plan periods, the expansion needed in the field of elementary education has been tremendous. But it goes without saying that the resources is very limited at our disposal. An extreme view of economization has also been adopted. India's Late Prime Minister, who was deeply concerned about this problem suggested open air school system. He suggested, "Can we not stop putting up any building in rural areas and devote the money thus saved to a better class of teachers as well as to some equipment?" He suggested opening elementary schools under simple sheds, while the actual class is done under trees. He further supported his scheme by saying, "Our climate helps and it is better to sit outside under a tree or a grove except during the rainy season. Also our old tradition fit in with this open-air teaching."

A correct assessment was made by Late Maulana Abul Kalam Azad in his presidential address to the 25th meeting of the Central Advisory Board of Education. He expressed almost similar views,

"Our climate is such that for a large part of the year, classes can be held in the open. If school holidays synchronies with the monsoons, we can to a large extent reduce the need for full-scale buildings. We can also economise by using simpler methods of construction for school purposes. From the earliest time rural India lived in mud bamboo or thatched houses. There is no reason why schools also should not be housed similarly." So, Late Maulana Azad had emphasised that whatever funds available must be devoted to the spread of education rather than the construction of buildings. Really the view is more tenable. The country under the circumstances should not go for pukka buildings with full accommodation. The school can have kacha buildings with some essential accommodation—a few class rooms, a store room, the teacher's room and the like. The villagers may be appealed to get involved in maintaining and repairing these buildings. In overcoming the shortage of funds the villagers are to be supplied with materials to build school houses in the same pattern, as the houses in which they live.

The idea of open-air school system is not bad, but it has certain limitations. That in many regions of the country the climate is so very unfavourable that open-air schooling becomes simply difficult, in some parts of the year. That some covered space is needed for sheltering school apparatus, books and furniture and also to organise craft work.

Shri K.G. Saiyidain, the Educational Advisor to the Govt. of India has observed that in the matter of school buildings there have been two schools of thought. One school pleads for impressive buildings, while the other favours "one-area-one-school" approach. There is much to be said in the existing conditions, not only on financial but also on educational grounds. It is a feeling of one section of people that school building should stand out in the village or the town as something of which the local community can be proud. While a majority group of people plead for keeping education close to nature, for teaching children not within the confines of small, cramped and dingy school rooms but in the open air.

Shri K.G. Saiyidain has presented a still better scheme, called by him, "Nucleus First Scheme". It is starting the school building with a nucleus and then proceeding by stages for expansion according to the needs. He goes against the concept of open air school system on various grounds. He goes against the concept of open-air school system, a functionally designed school room will provide sheltered space for storage etc. according to this Nucleus Scheme. At the same time the classes will be held outside. Shri Saiyidain has suggested two plans under this scheme. Nucleus First type school for two teachers. In this plan, we can build a pucca room of suitable size and partition into two rectangular parts. The diagram of such plan given below has been reproduced from "Schools For All" published by Ministry of Education, Govt. of India, 1958.

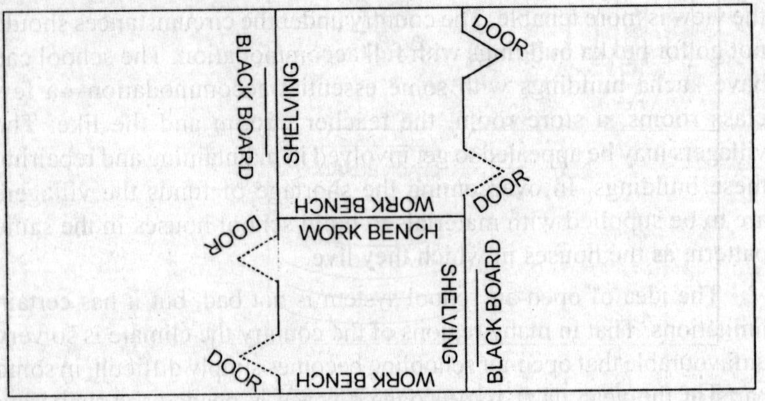

Nucleus First Type for Four Teachers

This plan consists of constructing a square room of suitable size. This is to be partitioned diagonally into four equals isosceles triangles. Each triangular room so formed at the central region, will have two openings on the outside with a black-board between the two openings (doors) will give storage space for equipment; craft tools, materials and various other teaching aids. The classes will sit in the open making use of the chalk-boards.

This Nucleus can thus provide excellent facilities for four classes or grades in an Elementary School. The spaces X_1, X_2, X_3, and X_4 between the classes will be used by the class for activities, like gardening, planting and other craft works. Here the Nucleus is divided into four parts. The black-board is placed at the corner and the pupils sit in semi-circular rows facing the black-board. Light comes from behind and there is full protection from rain.

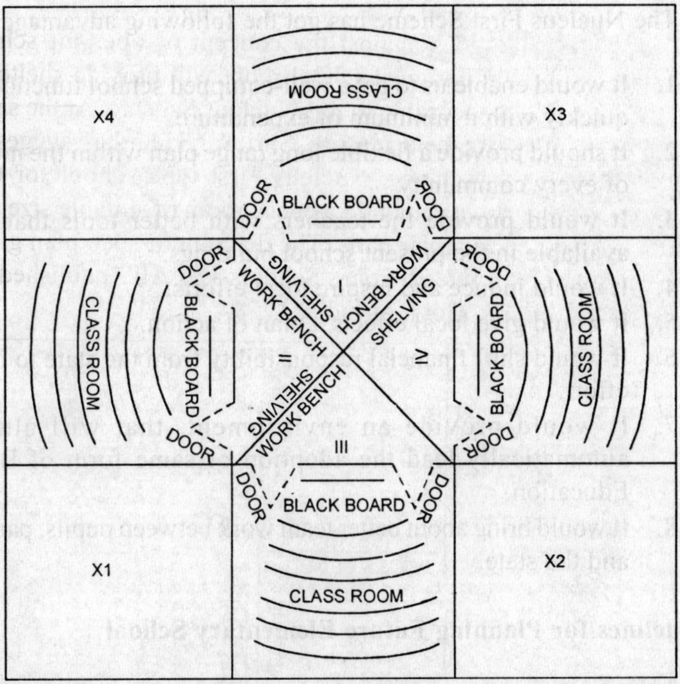

The Nucleus First Scheme was also approved by our Late Prime Minister. Mr. Nehru. In this regard he expressed the following view: "For my part I would start school without any building. In the final analysis, it is the trained doctor or nurse who is important for establishment of clinics and health centres. We think much of the building and forget the human aspect. We should think of simple type of buildings, forgetting the PWD standards which are not satisfactory and practical. The Education Department should get away from the rut of PWD. We should have a cheap building with a room say 20' × 20' or 25' × 25' divided diagonally into four parts. The room would serve as an equipment room and not a classroom. Each of the four walls should have outside a black-board and teaching will go on in all the four directions outside these walls. If necessary a platform and shade may be provided and gradually pucca buildings may come into existence through village cooperation. We have to adopt these things to our conditions and make them cheap, so that we can concentrate of giving more equipment and wages".

The Nucleus First Scheme has got the following advantages:

1. It would enable us to get a well-equipped school functioning quickly with a minimum of expenditure.
2. It should provide a flexible long range plan within the means of every community.
3. It would provide the teachers with better tools than are available in the present school buildings.
4. It would induce and inspire local efforts.
5. It would give local effects a plan of action.
6. It would shift financial responsibility from the state to local effort.
7. It would provide an environment, that will almost automatically lead the adoption of same form of Basic Education.
8. It would bring about better team work between pupils, parents and the state.

Guidelines for Planning Future Elementary School

(i) A master plan should be drawn up for the site as a whole, so that future development is smooth,
(ii) The first step is construction of the Nucleus.
(iii) As the members grow, the Nucleus should be repeated.
(iv) The shelters for the classroom should be provided by the community.
(v) In course of time, quarters should be prepared for the teachers and prepare plan for capital outlay in advance.
(vi) To cope with increasing numbers, two shifts should be introduced in the same building.

Planning and Designing for Secondary School

General Principles

1. Always it is advisable to have the buildings of one story. The second can be erected in future when further expansion is needed.

2. The building at secondary level should be pucca rather than kacha. The most important rooms must be pucca and the less important rooms, like store, cycle-shed, servant room etc. may be kacha.
3. The building must be planned with hygienic laws. Full attention must be given to site, soil, area, ventilation, lighting and other allied problems.
4. The planning and designing should be scientific and modern. Corridors should be wide enough to avoid congestion when classes change. Verandahs should be provided adjacent to the rooms to aid free movement of students. The Latrines and Urinals should be a little a way form the rooms, but easily accessible.
5. There should be adequate washing and laboratory arrangements. Water-taps providing fresh drinking water must be located at a suitable place easily accessible to the public. The flash latrines should be provided, one for 50 children.
6. Adequate space must be provided with classroom, special rooms, school halls, staff room, office room, pupils' common room, library and reading room in every secondary school. Class room should have 600 sq. ft, floor area (30' × 20'). The height of each room must be more than 15 feet.
7. Efforts should be made to have school buildings with a graceful look, because "the exterior will suggest and reflect the character of the interior".
8. As regards the type of the design, no single type can be recommended. The different types of designs that are in vogue for secondary schools are:
   (i) The I Type—Consisting of a row of classrooms.
   (ii) The L Type—I type with an extension on the side.
   (iii) The T Type—I type with extension on the side both ways.
   (iv) The U Type—Two I's joined on one aide.

The above types of designs will not suit a multipurpose school which by its very nature is supposed to provide a number of elective

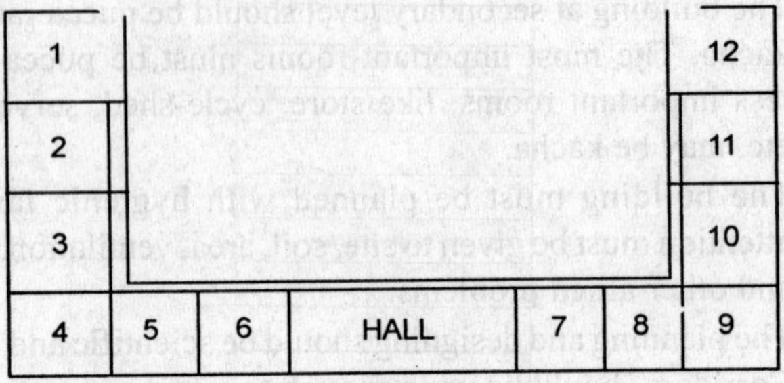

"U" TYPE

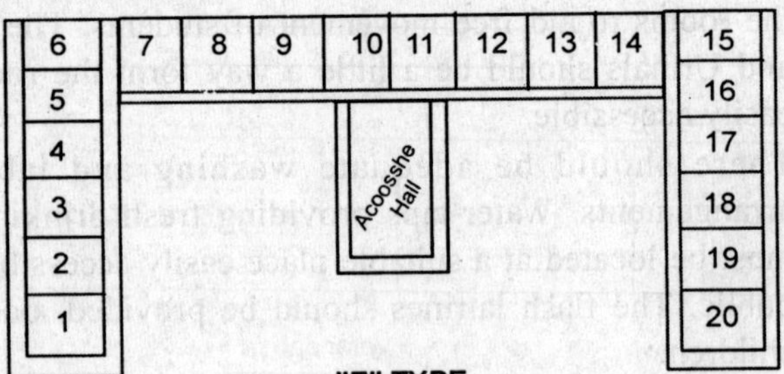

"E" TYPE

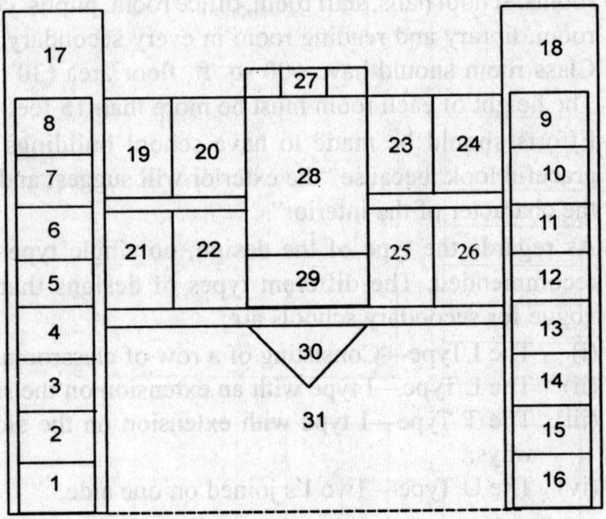

The H Type

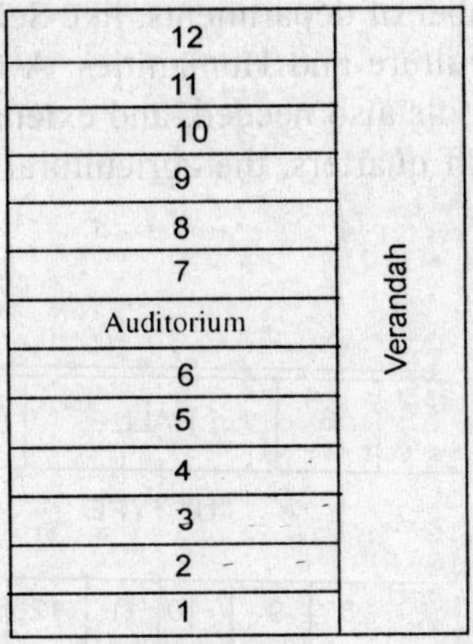

"T" Type Building

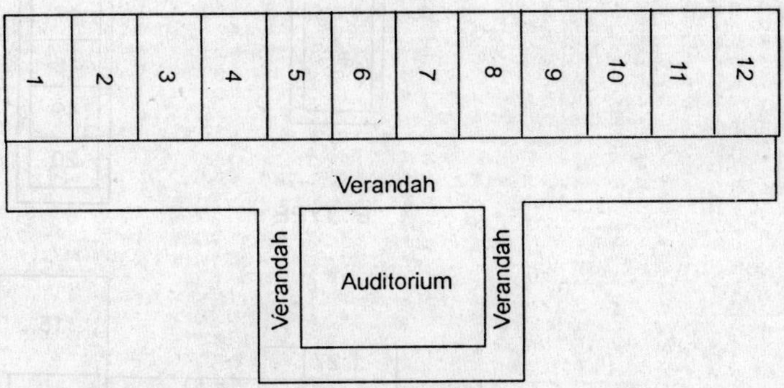

"T" Type Building

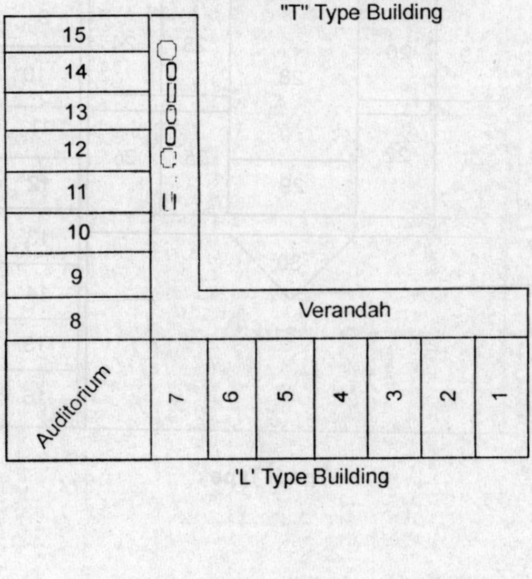

'L' Type Building

groups and a number of departments, like Science, Technology, Art, Commerce, Agriculture and Humanities. A full-fledged residential multipurpose schools also needed, and extension campus with hall, the hostel, the staff quarters, the agricultural farm, the play ground and the like.

16

Role of Headmasters and Teachers

Headmaster

In the planning and execution of school programme, the head of the institution, teachers, students and their parents have all to join hands to attain common goals and purposes. The Headmaster may be described as the Solar Orb, round whom all the teacher planets revolve. A better analogy is given by W.M. Ryburn, when he compares the Headmaster to the Captain of a ship, who like Captain in the ship, holds the key position in the school. Ryburn wants a Headmaster to be a man of faith. It is therefore, essential that he is not only a man of high character, but a man of faith, "Faith in vocation, faith in his pupils, faith in human nature and faith in his staff'. Also Ryburn lays emphasis on the inspiring qualities of the Headmaster of the schools. "He must also be able to inspire the staff in their day-to-day work, inspire pupils to use all opportunities provided, drawing out the best that is in them inspire the society."

In the worlds of the Central Advisory Board of Education, "No scheme of educational reconstruction will produce the desired result, unless it is administered with vision and efficiency. The person who plans with vision and executes with responsibility is virtually the headmaster". In fact, school is the lengthened shadow of Headmaster.

The Secondary Education Commission (1952-53) opines on Headmaster, "On him the proper working of school ultimately depends the reputation of the school and the position that it holds in the society depends in a large measure on the influence that he exercises over his colleagues, his pupils and general public.

True, on his ability and skill, as a sound and effective educational leader depends the success of a school system. A Headmaster is the leader and the centre of the whole organisation of the school. P.C. Wren beautifully explains the role of the Headmaster in the following world:

> "What the mainspring is to the watch, the fly-wheel to the machine, or the engine to steamship, the Headmaster is to the school. The character of the school reflects and proclaims the professional character of the Headmaster. He is the seal and the school is the wax."

"As the Headmaster, so is the school". There is no denying the fact that everything in the school, the staff, the curriculum, the method of instruction, the discipline, the co-curricular, activities, the daily schedule and the general atmosphere and the tone of the school is fashioned in the mould of the Headmaster. It may be recalled that some schools in England are still named after their reputed Headmaster, i.e. Harrow School, Rugby importance in the school programme. The whole programme of school either grows or remains sterile according to equipment, training and competence of the Headmaster. Everything in the school, buildings, furniture, library, laboratory, methods & techniques of teaching, co-curricular activities and human relationships bear the impact of the personality of the head and reflect his leadership.

The role of the Headmaster as a man is perhaps the most important. He is both trustful trustworthy. He should always carry a young heart.

An Ideal Headmaster

He is academically and professionally well-equipped. He must possess progressive outlook and constructive leadership. An ideal headmaster recognises that a good organisation is an arrangement of persons, wherein its members may work effectively, economically and harmoniously together to achieve a common purpose. The Headmaster must be cultured, well-behaved. He must be social and sociable. He should be able to win confidence and earn respect of others.

The good Headmaster is the leader of school. He should have a clear perception of ideals of education. He must possess ability to coordinate the work of the human equipment of the school. He should not be parasite of public funds.

Really, an ideal Headmaster is sensitive to the needs of the society. He may be able to transform schools into free and cooperative communities of youth. He must have a good knowledge communities of youth. He must have a good knowledge of child and adolescent psychology, general principles of health and hygiene, the latest trends and practices in education. The Headmaster cannot be expected to be the master of all subjects, but he has to plan, organise and supervise instructional work at school. He must familiarize with methods of teaching different subjects, should make discussions with different subject teachers about problems experienced in their subject areas. So it is ideal to possess a sort of mastery over fundamentals of different school subjects.

In brief, the headmaster must have well-developed personality He must look a man of maturity and wisdom. He must be able to make favourable impression upon all. He cannot afford to be careless even about his dress and manners. He may not have the traditional cane in his hand in order to maintain discipline in the school.

Headmaster's Relation

Headmaster occupies a key position in the school and the social environment around. His personal reputation and the reputation of the school depends mostly upon the relation that he maintains with the staff, students, their parents and the community.

1. *Relation with Staff:* A Headmaster must be sympathetic towards the members of staff. He should rule with love and kindness rather than authority and order. A Headmaster with a despotic and autocratic behaviour is bound to meet with failure in the present democratic set-up. The Headmaster must respect the personality of teachers and recognize their worth. He should not consider himself as a superhuman person, a divine leader of people. He should not maintain an air of superiority of false dignity. The Headmaster should forget the principles, "King can do no wrong", "I am the monarch of all I survey",

"I am the school", etc. He should equate himself with others and remember the ladder by which he ascended. He should have tolerance and breadth of heart. He should forgive them for minor mistake and trifling lapses. He should not allow the teachers to get frustrated and must cheer them up whenever they are in difficulty. The Headmaster should abstain from negative methods of maintaining discipline, such as threat, detection, system of spies, secret reporting, dividing the staff in mutually antagonistic groups etc.

The Headmaster must recognize the individual difference in order to allot work to the staff in accordance with their capacities and abilities. He should be judicious in assigning duties and issuing orders and should not expect anything more from the teachers than their ability, interest, aptitude and previous achievement. A particular teacher may be best fitted for writing the annual report, but not making the seating arrangement at the annual function. The Headmaster should see that a square peg is put in a square hole.

He must seek advice from teachers and bring them into confidence. In this way he will create a sense of belongingness among them. The leader of a school can be successful only when he secures willing cooperation from his co-workers, when he makes those co-workers feel that the problems of the school are theirs and not his own.

The Headmaster must organise staff meetings and discuss various matters regarding planning the school work, organising activities and distribution of labour. Group mind is more fertile than individual mind, and so group action is more fruitful than individual action taken by a Headmaster.

2. *Relation with Pupils:* Great Headmasters have been great friends of pupils. The distance between the two must be narrowed down to the limits of maintaining both intimacy and prestige. Dignity actually does not consist in aloofness and in maintaining an air of superiority. Rather it consists in being helpful and in doing right thing in the right time.

The Headmaster should take keen interest in the welfare of students. He must look after their studies, home-work, participation in various activities, their physical health, their comforts in the hostel and even in their dress, diet and rest. He should give free access to them so that they approach him with request and problems. He may meet them in the class, in the playfield, in the hostel and talk to them freely. He must try to know as many students as possible by name. There are Headmaster, who work in the field with students, who play with them, who treat them like friends and who give them a number of facilities like easy entry into the Headmaster's office, use of telephone etc.

3. *Relation with Parents:* Headmaster is the coordinating agency between the parents and the schools. He should exploit direct and indirect contact, indirectly by sending progress reports, circulars and inviting suggestions from them about school improvement. As per direct contact, the Headmaster should assign specific hours for interview with parents and guardians, invite them to school functions and should convene the frequent parent-teacher meets.

Most important is the dialogue or conversation between Headmaster and the parents. The Headmaster should not feel irritate over exaggerated complaint of parents against the school. Any way, he' should earn good-will and whole-hearted co-operation of the parents rather than resentment and indifference. Parent-cum-officers should help the school to progress.

4. *Relation with the Community:* School is a social institution, so it is a centre of community life. The Headmaster should know what the community expects the school to do. He should exploit all the community resources for the benefit of school.

The Headmaster should invite the members of the community to witness school exhibitions, dramatic performances, variety shows and other activities organised by the school. He himself should address various clubs and organisations of the community

Duties and Functions of Headmaster

As is the Headmaster, so is the school. In his duties and function, he has to be sweet and soft as well as still and stern. As a functionary, hundreds and thousands of eyes watch him, judge him, measure him and eager to follow his noble examples. Unless he has a perceiving eye, and understanding heart and an all-adjusting mental poise, he is bound to falter and fumble in his duties. The Headmaster should be firm in his dealings, resolute in his conviction and decisions, relentless in his execution.

A Headmaster has to perform multifarious duties. They can be categorised conveniently into the following:

(a) *Teaching:* Headmaster of a school is a teacher first and last. Teaching is his fundamental duty. Headmasters remain so much absorbed in other duties that they never enter classes. But they should take at least two periods a day on specialised subjects. They should deliver or guide demonstration classes. Despite some frustration of administration and demands on his time improvement of instruction is one of the most important responsibilities and duties of Headmaster. The headmastership and leadership are synonymous in education. He is the key person charged with responsibilities of improving instruction.

By actually teaching, the Headmaster comes to know the standard of pupils in different classes and the standard of teaching in the school. He directly comes in contact and understands difficulties of students and teachers.

No one expects Headmaster to be an expert in all instructional areas. He may master at least one or two subjects with manageable standard in other subjects. In spite of the fact, that Headmasters are over-burdened with a number of other duties, they should be first rate teachers being conversant with content and the latest methods of teaching.

(b) *Planning:* Unless the Headmaster plans for the school, there will be confusion all round. For making proper planning, help of pupils, teachers, parents should be taken. Most of the planning will be there in course of discussions of school problems in the staff meetings and students councils. Jacobson paints a good picture, "In extreme cases there are teachers without students, classes without teacher, class-sections with enrolment twice the capacity of the room, the teachers are handicapped, because of shortage of suppliers, lack of books and equipments, improperly classified students". This state of affairs is due to inadequate planning in schools.

(c) *Organisation and Administration:* The next important task of Headmaster is organisation. In the organisation of school plant the headmaster should procure adequate furniture and equipment for the school. He should make petty repairs, distribute the furniture, look to the buildings, organise laboratories, the workshop and the library and take care of the sanitation and entire material aspect of school plant. The Headmaster looks to the instructional work of the school including construction of curriculum, preparation and distribution at syllabi, work distribution among the staff, allotment of co-curricular duties, construction of the time schedule and the school calendar.

(d) *Supervision:* Supervision and administration are the two combined functions which are mostly blended in one. Administration means performance of certain routine duties in connection with finance, discipline, correspondence etc. By supervision it is meant the overseeing the work done by the teaching staff. Supervision is improving the total teaching-learning situation. This situation is no more "detection or fault finding". A Headmaster should follow the following principles of supervision:

1. Its purpose is to help, encourage and guide rather than criticise.
2. It should be done in a spirit of cooperation.
3. It should be done regularly and effectively.
4. Partiality and prejudice should find no place in it.
5. The criteria of supervision should be known to teachers.

Supervision of instructional work is the most important function of the Headmaster. Classroom is the heart of teaching situation. It is the centre of instruction. It is the duty of Headmaster to upgrade the quality of education through creative, cooperative and constructive supervision. It is not a matter of rushing into a classroom in session to make correction or an adjustment, as an auto mechanic adjusts a faulty motor. A motor is a thing within itself, but a classroom is a combination of human beings. Class visits form an essential part of the duties of the Headmaster. But that alone given him no right either to snub or criticise a teacher in the presence of the class.

If the Headmaster feels a particular teacher needs correction, he should send for the teacher for post-visit conference. So, Headmaster's role is to play an excellent guide and the post-visit conference should see the teacher, a better person, wiser and saner. When Headmaster finds any defect with the teacher, he will discuss after the period is over in the Headmaster's office and not in front of the class.

Some Specific Duties of Headmaster

1. *School Supplies: This* involves planning. Estimates are to be prepared regarding the quantity of purchases to be made. Specification of each item is to be laid down and quotations have to be invited and approved by the Headmaster. Goods ordered should be inspected and checked on arrival. Headmaster will appoint a selection committee for purchase and maintenance of equipments. This committee will prepare the list of items of purchase.
2. *School Campus:* School plant should provide adequate educational services. Best use of all the rooms, laboratories, workshops and the farm be made. In case of over-crowding students may attend laboratories in groups. School may be used for its specific uses. All school buildings should be guarded against building hazards. The perfect up-keep of the school campus is the lookout of the Headmaster.
3. *Co-Curricular Activities:* Over-all management of school co-curricular activities is the Headmaster's responsibility. Various activities may of course, be distributed amongst the staff members in accordance with their previous background, interest and aptitude. Adequate budget allotment should be made for these activities. All wastage and unnecessary expenditure should be checked.
4. *Office*: The modern conception of the Headmaster's office is that, it is a service centre. Communication with higher authorities, the parents, the public, the teacher and the students is made by the Headmaster.

Among the specific duty on the Headmaster in respect of efficient working of school office, the following are noteworthy:

(i) The office must be located at a suitable place. It must be adequately spaced and proper up-keep ensured.

(ii) Office work must be distributed adequately among members of the office staff. Headmaster must supervise their work, check irregularities, check inefficiency and ensure regular and prompt work.

(iii) Headmaster must decide time to be devoted for office work.

(iv) Headmaster must make note of his office duties.

(v) Duties of Headmaster prescribed by Education Department and Managing Committee should be strictly followed.

(vi) The Headmaster should strictly obey the rules and regulations by the University or School Board, to which the school is affiliated.

(vii) Routine duties of the Headmaster should be admission, checking class registers, cash book, acquaintance roll, attendance registers accounts of various fees and fines.

All these general duties and specific responsibilities of the Headmaster will go to make better schools.

THE TEACHER

Importance: No better tributes have been paid to any man on earth than to the teacher. East or West, everywhere he has been respected and worshipped. In the ancient India teacher was ranked next to God. In the West he is called, the "architect of nation", "maker of man", "the maker of history". Like the gardener, the caresses young human beings and looks after their physical, mental and social growth and development. It is said that God has created man after his own image, the teacher fashions the child, after his own image. It goes, "As the teacher, so is the pupil". According to the Hindu point of views, the child receives second-birth at the hands of the teacher. First birth, the physical one front the parents. The teacher played the most prominent role in moulding the habits, tastes and the character of pupils. He turns the child from animality to specialised human form. Books may teach a child, but the teacher educates.

Manu the ancient Indian sage says, "A teacher is the image of Brahma, a father is the image of Prajapati, a mother is the image of Earth". The famous Indian prayer runs that "The teacher is Brahma, the creator, he is God Vishnu, he is God Maheswar. He is entire Universe, obeisance to teacher". Cicero said 2000 years ago: "What greater or better gift can we offer the republic than to teach and instruct our youth?" His word spoken in Greece about 2000 years ago holds true even today, truly the quality of a nation depends upon the quality of its teachers. Humayun Kabir says, "Teachers are literally the arbiters of a nation's destiny".

The Secondary Education Commission (1952-53) also points out "every teacher and educationist of experience knows that even the best curriculum and the most perfect syllabus remains dead unless quickened into life by the right methods of teaching and right kind of teachers".

The opening sentence of the Kothari Commission Report speaks very high of teachers, "the destiny of India is now being shaped in her classroom". Whether the teacher is in the best equipped room of a most up-to-date school, whether the teacher is at work with a small group of students or is on a television screen that is seen by tens of thousands; whether the teacher is a person or a programmed text-book, it is unlikely that the students will get superior education unless the teacher is superior. To this Mudaliar Commission Report has stated, "We are concerned that the important factor in the contemplated educational reconstruction is the teacher—his personal qualities, his education qualities, his professional training and the place that he occupies in the school as well as in the community."

Qualification from Different Points of View

1. Teacher is the most vital single factor in the system of education. It is the teacher, who matters most as far as the quality of education is concerned. Really, the well-equipped teacher is a supreme factor in education. The framers of the Second Five Year Plan observed, "At all times, the teacher is the pivot in the system of education. This is specially the case in a period of basic change and reorientation.
2. Teacher is the back bone of society. It is particularly so in remote village. He stands as an outstanding figure among the illiterate and semi-illiterate families. He is their friend, philosopher and guide.

3. Teacher is superior guide. At the back of every great man, a good teacher is there who kindled enthusiasm fostered confidence and guided him to the way of progress. A conqueror of the statue of Alexander the Great said, "I owe my birth to my father, but life to my teacher."
4. Teacher is the nation builder. Teacher shapes the children who are potential leaders of tomorrow.
5. A teacher affects eternity. Henry Adams stated so well "A parent gives life, but as parent, he gives no more. A murderer takes life, but his deed stops there. A teacher affects eternity, he can never tell when his influence stops."
6. Teachers should command respect. Pupils have their likes and dislikes. They feel that teachers must be human, friendly and "One of us." They should be good natured, jolly, with sense of humour and should not demand respect from their students.
7. According to the Headmaster, the teachers should be obedient to duty, hardworking, intelligent, cooperative and hopeful. They should try for best results and to raise the status of their school.
8. Parents like the teachers to be highly sympathetic to the child paying individual attention.
9. The higher educational authorities have their own whims. Judging teachers from examination results standpoint, they try to punish teachers with a view to setting them right. They want teachers to-be meek and humble. They want also teachers to work under the worst conditions. The teachers should be resourceful even if they are asked to work in adverse conditions of poor house accommodation, ill-equipped classrooms even without a black-board. The authorities should sincerely try their best to improve the lot of such teacher.
10. The educationists have given a long list of traits and qualities essential for a good teacher. Teacher is also a man, he is not a superhuman being.
11. Teachers must possess a devotion to profession with a strong sense of vocation, teachers should go for a true devotion to

teaching. He must work in a missionary zeal. He must be somewhat prepared to sacrifice his self in the cause of education. The famous Sanskrit Poet of India, Kalidas says, "If the teachers scholarship is just earning bread, then he is no better than a shop-keeper selling knowledge".

12. Once a teacher, always a teacher should be the motto. He must not oscillate and make teaching a stepping-stone to other vocations. A renowned educationist remarks, "the strength of school depends upon the permanency of its teachers. If teachers to look teaching merely as a step-gap until they get something better, then it is the school that suffers". So teachers should consider teaching a calling and not a trade.

TEACHER'S RELATION WITH OTHERS

A. Teacher and his Pupils

(i) It is said, "A teacher is in locoparent is (the second parent)". He must know the child fully well. The teacher's work is to discover student's abilities, interests, aptitudes, likes and dislikes. There should be no scope to misunderstand the child. And in order to understand the child he may have to come down to' the level of the child. The teacher should not hesitate to mix freely with the child.

(ii) The teacher must understand the child, he should sympathise with his fundamental needs and take genuine interest in him.

(iii) Teacher's behaviour with child should neither be stern and rigid so as to make himself unapproachable. He must himself not rule by fear. India's Late President Dr. Zakir Hussain says, "The teacher's task is not to dictate or dominate, he is to help and serve to understand and shape in faith, love, and reverence — yes reverence for the child. Teachers like these can be trusted in our Indian education which alone can bring about the change in our society".

(iv) He must shun 19th century egotism, false dignity and vanity. He should be able to come down to the level of the pupils. No rebukes should be on there his tongue, and no cane in his hand.

(v) His behaviour should be exemplary. He must act as a model for the pupils and must do nothing himself that he forbids his pupils to do. He must avoid smoking, drinking, gambling, spitting, quarrelling etc. and all such unworthy actions.

(vi) He must be able to inspire the pupils to learn more and more. It is well said, there are no dull and hard subjects, there are only dull and hard teachers.

(vii) Tact is another word for common sense. The teacher should be tactful in his dealings with the pupils. He must make judicious use of praise and blame. He must sometimes pat them and sometimes pull them by ears.

(viii) He should neither flatter nor be amenable to flatterer.

(ix) The teacher must pay individual attention towards backward, abnormal and problem students. Nobody should feel neglected at his hands.

(x) Teacher should be firm believer in fair dealings. Any display of favouritism is detrimental to the best interests of the pupils. The teacher is not only an instructor and taskmaster, he is a helper and guide to the students.

B. Teacher's Relation with Colleagues

(i) Teaching is a cooperative enterprise. So a teacher must be able to pull on well with the members of the staff as family members. He should avoid back-biting, unnecessary interference in the tasks assigned to others, criticism of teaching ability of others, untoward behaviour towards colleagues in the presence of pupils. The teacher should be tolerant. He should refrain from speaking ill of a fellow teacher. A desire for self-aggrandizement is to be deplored.

(ii) A teacher out of frustration may criticise the school system in which he works. The older teacher need not fear criticism from young co-workers and the beginners should develop an attitude of respect towards the older colleagues. There are some teachers who carry tales to one teacher against another. This should be discouraged for good of all concerned.

C. Teacher's Attitude Towards Superiors

(i) Teachers must work with headmaster or inspecting officer in a spirit of friends understanding and cooperation. Sometimes the headmaster or supervisor creates unhealthy reactions in the minds of the teachers through deliberate partiality and prejudices. Still the teachers should show some breadth of vision and toleration in accommodating the superior officers.

(ii) The teacher may feel irritated over petty matters when he is asked to do a particular work in a particular way that he does not like. He may not able to appreciate the decision of the headmaster and may hold quite opposite views still he should try to have perfect understanding with his superiors.

(iii) The teacher should not entertain any secret hostility and should not say anything dishonouring the headmaster. Even in the staff meetings, he may express difference of opinion but once the decisions have been arrived at it is his moral binding to carry out the decisions.

D. Teachers and Parents

(i) Teachers should have intimate relationship with the parents in the interest of pupils. Teacher may know the pupil better if he knows his parents and his family background. So he should take all measures to have a better contact with the parents of students.

(ii) It is the duty of teachers to educate parents also. He should arrange special lectures, film show, exhibition etc. in the school where the parents should be invited.

(iii) The teacher should understand the financial position of the parents. The teacher should help the students in providing financial aids, scholarships, medical aids and in procuring books, papers and stationeries at concessional rates.

E. Teacher and Community

(i) The school springs from the community and works to enrich it. The teacher should re-establish this much forgotten relationship.

(ii) The teacher should not entertain the wrong notion that community has nothing to contribute to the school substantially. If the teacher is resourceful, he can approach the local Doctor, the engineer, the postmaster, the carpenter or weaver and tap the resources of such society members for the benefit of school. The teacher should establish fullest contact with the community. He should make the school a community centre.

Work-Load Distribution of Teachers

Almost in all schools, distribution of work poses a problem. Very few headmasters know the principles of distribution of workload among the teaching staff. There is a sort of hierarchy of subjects as regards strain involved in an ascending order. The Science and Mathematics teachers take much more strain than those who teach History, Geography or Languages. A Mathematics teacher after solving a number of questions will perspire more than a language teacher who may enjoy piece of poem. So the strain becomes gradually less, who take up craft, art and music or physical education or other co-curricular activities.

In some big schools there are sections in different classes. Here the teachers take less strain. 40 pupils is the convenient number in a section. In some states it goes up to 45 or 50. In some schools, the number in a section becomes 55 even. So the teacher is involved in a heavy size of correction work in every week. Again such load becomes proportionately heavier when the school goes understaffed. More periods involve more strain. More so, few teachers are there who are really devotees of teaching to take any strain. Dr. K.L. Shrimali in his pamphlet, "Better teacher education" makes an accurate study of situation. "A general survey of the teaching profession will reveal that a large majority of teachers do not cater this profession by choice, but are forced into it by circumstances. It will also be found that people who go into the profession come mostly from families belonging to lower income groups in the community". So the teaching staff in India rarely come from the upper strata of society with their brilliant academic achievements and job satisfaction.

A well-known headmaster V.S. Mathur remarks, "Unless we improve substantially the quality of teaching force and see only men or women fitted by temperament, character, intelligence or aptitude for teaching are allowed to become teachers. We shall look in vain for any reform in education".

Present Conditions of Teachers

Education is the back-bone of progressing nation and teacher is the pivot in the system of education. It is obvious, the progress of a nation depends upon the qualities of its teachers. Every where it is acclaimed that the teaching profession is the noblest of all professions. But it is the irony of fate that teaching is the most unattractive profession and the teacher, no longer occupies and honourable position in society. The teacher in India today, "suffers from poverty, neglect, indifference and insecurity." Financially they are poor, socially their status is low, professionally their task is a permanent dissatisfaction and administratively they are worst affected. Prof. K.G. Saiyidain rightly observed that "teaching is still an unattractive profession which many persons take up at a last resort".

CUMULATIVE RECORD CARDS

A cumulative record is a systematic account of information about a student. It is an evaluation tool which presents a comprehensive record of the achievement or otherwise of each student in different aspect—physical, academic, moral, social and health. It begins as soon as the child enters the school and continues till he leaves the school. The information written in the cumulative record cards are collected from different sources over a period of time.

Need of the Cumulative Record Card

The Cumulative Record Card of a student is needed for the following important points.

1. To give a complete picture of a pupil's all round progress in different areas i.e. physical, academic, moral, social and health.
2. To assess the child, his potentialities, interest, aptitude and talents.
3. To provide proper guidance and counselling taking into consideration of students curricular and co-curricular achievements.
4. To help parents and teachers in the placement of pupil after the completion of schooling/study.

Content of a Cumulative Record Card (CRC)

The Cumulative Record Card records the following information regarding different aspects of pupils development.

1. *Personal data* — Personal data give introductory information about a child like his name, sex, date of birth, age, permanent address, parents name and family background.
2. *Academic data* —It deals with the information about the previous schools attended earlier, present grade or class, roll number, examinations appeared, results, division and percentage of marks in each examination failures, percentage of attendance etc.
3. *Health data* — It reveals information regarding height, weight, blood pressure, communicable diseases if any, treatments given, food habits, exercise parental disease if any, care taken if handicap etc.
4. *Co-curricular activities data* — The child's participation in different co-curricular activities, leadership qualities, certificates awarded, prizes and medals received are recorded in it.
5. *Personality characteristics* — This reveals the psychological aspects like intellectual ability self-confidence, emotional stability, leadership qualities, tolerance, initiative and sense of responsibility etc.
6. *Record of counselling and guidance* — The problems found

with the child, date of interview, reasons discovered, remedial measures taken, following programmes etc. are mentioned in the card.

7. *General over all Remarks* — General remarks by the class teacher and Headmaster on the performance and talents of the pupil.

Guidelines for Maintaining Cumulative Record Card

1. The teachers should be in-charge of maintaining cumulative records. He should make the entries up-to-date.
2. Required information should be collected from various persons like parents, friends, subject teachers and child himself by different techniques.
3. Different techniques should be used to collect information about a child i.e. psychological tests, observations by teachers, examination result etc.
4. The teachers in-charge of maintaining cumulative records should be given proper orientation and training about how to maintain it.
5. Secret or confidential matters should find a place in it but a separate file may be made for such entries.
6. The guidance worker of the school should be in overall charge of maintenance of cumulative records.
7. Cumulative record cards maintenance should be supervised by the Headmaster and Inspector of Schools.

17

Organisation of Curricular and Co-curricular Activities

After Independence, the University Education Commission (1948-49) in course of their investigations found the Secondary Education to be "the weakest link" between Elementary and University Education in India. As per this Commission's suggestions, Secondary Education Commission (1952-53) was appointed, which laid down the following:

(i) The present curriculum is narrowly conceived,
(ii) It is bookish and theoretical,
(iii) It is over-crowded without providing rich and significant contents,
(iv) It makes inadequate provision for practical and other kinds of activities which should reasonably find room in it, if it is to educate the whole of the personality,
(v) It does not cater to the various needs and capacities of the adolescents,
(vi) It is dominated too much by examinations, and
(vii) It does not include technical vocational subjects which are so necessary for training the students to take part in the industrial and economic development of the country.

The Commission of Education and National Development (1964-66) has stated that the school curriculum is in a state of flux all over the world today. In developing countries it is generally criticised as being inadequate and outmoded and not properly designed to meet the needs of modern times. Even in an educationally advanced nation like the U.S.A. where the traditional curriculum had been radically transformed long ago under the impact of progressive education, the content of the school courses is being challenged by several scholars and University men and new reform movement has been started which may bring in sweeping curricular changes in school education". The Education Commission has said, "We conceive of the school curriculum as the totality of learning experience that the school provides for the pupils through all the manifold activities in the school or outside that are carried on under its supervision. From this point of view, the distinction between curricular and co-curricular work ceases to exist, and a school camp and games and sports are curricular or rather co-curricular activities. There are, however, certain activities of this type such as hobbies of different kinds, debates, dramas which have more of the quality of play than of work and which give greater opportunities for creative self-expression. Every school should organize a variety of such programmes so that every child in it may be able to take up something suited to his tastes and interests".

Curriculum at Different Stages

(a) *Lower Primary Stage (Classes I-IV):* The child should receive instruction in the basic tools of learning such as reading, writing and computation and should learn to adjust to his surrounding through an elementary study of his physical and social environment. For a sound foundation of mother-tongue, no language other than this should be introduced during the first four years. The curriculum should be gradually expanded and developed in keeping with the child's growth and development.

The curriculum at this stage should include:

(i) One language, the mother-tongue or the regional language,

(ii) Arithmetic,

(iii) Study of the environment (covering Science and Social Studies in classes III and IV),

(iv) Creative activities,

(v) Work-experience and Social Service, and

(vi) Health education.

(b) *Higher Primary Stage (Classes V-VII)*: The study of second language will be added to mother-tongue; arithmetic skill will be used in acquisition of more difficult mathematical knowledge; environmental activities will lead to the study of natural and physical sciences, history, geography and civics. The constructive and creative skills will provide the basis for the practice of simple acts and crafts. And the practice of healthy living will serve as foundation for physical education. At this stage the curriculum will cover the following:

(i) Two language; Mother-tongue and Hindi or English; it is to be noted that a third language (English, Hindi or a regional language) may be introduced on an optional basis,

(ii) Mathematics,

(iii) General Science,

(iv) Social Studies (History, Geography and Civics),

(v) Art,

(vi) Work Experience and Social Service,

(vii) Physical Education, and

(viii) Education in Moral and Spiritual values.

(c) *Secondary Stage:* The curriculum should meet the needs of the adolescent individuals as well as the democratic society in which the child is expected to participate as a citizen on reaching maturity. The secondary school curriculum should contain necessary educational elements for cultivation of certain skills, elements, attitudes, and qualities of character viz. capacity for clear thinking, the ability to communicate easily with his fellowmen, a sense of true patriotism and an appreciation of the value of productive work. The needs of adolescence are related not only to the acquisition of knowledge and the promotion of intellectual ability, but the fuller development of physical, emotional, aesthetic and moral aspects of personality. Provision has, therefore, to be made in the curriculum for the programme of physical education. At this stage (classes VIII-X) the curriculum should include:

(i) Three languages: Mother-tongue, Hindi and English in non-Hindi area and in Hindi area mother-tongues (Hindi). English and one of the 15 modern Indian languages other than Hindi, it may here be noted the a classical language may be studied in addition to the above 3 languages on an optional basis.

(ii) Mathematics,

(iii) General Science,

(iv) History, Geography and Civics,

(v) Art,

(vi) Work-experience and Social Service,

(vii) Physical education, and education in moral and spiritual values.

(d) *Subject Areas of Higher Secondary (+2) Course:* The existing one year higher-secondary course will soon cover a two-year period after the 10 years schooling pattern. The whole question of higher secondary curriculum will have to be carefully examined and details worked out by an expert body consisting of representatives of the Universities, State Board of School Education and State Department of Education. The curriculum will cover a large area than that of the 10 year pattern of curriculum as follows:

(i) Any two Indian languages including MIL English and any classical language,

(ii) Any three subjects from among History, Geography, Economics, Logic, Psychology, Sociology, Art, Physics, Chemistry, Mathematics, Biology, Geology, Home Science and an additional language,

(iii) Work-experience and Social Service,

(iv) Physical Education,

(v) Art and Craft, and

(vi) Education on Moral and Spiritual value.

ORGANISATION OF CO-CURRICULAR ACTIVITIES

Meaning and Origin: Co-curricular activities now considered as the intrinsic part of the endeavour in a school. Till lately they were being called as extra-curricular activities. But now theses have been recognised as a part of regular curriculum for the complete education of the child. In fact, curricular and co-curricular activities are considered complementary to each other, both deserving equal weight and emphasis in the total programme of school. Co-curricular activities form a vital link in the pattern of blended educational experiences, so necessary for all boys and girls in the modern Indian schools. These educative experiences comprise all experiences inside as well as outside the class room, to overall facets of growth pattern. They ensure balanced development of the child which aims at good citizenship for the country. So the distinction between curricular and co-curricular must cease to exists.

The so-called curricular activities have deep roots in the ancient system of education in India. Each disciple in the Ashram or Gurukula had to fetch wood from the jungle, to attained to kitchen-gardening and also to perform physical work. Archery was a compulsory activity of Kshatriya students. A pupil working with his own hands was considered pure and clean. As early as 400 B.C. in ancient Greece no less importance was given to clubs; discussion groups, debating games, dramatics etc. were actively encouraged by the teachers in Sparta. The Spartian aim of education was development of strong, well-built, and healthy citizens always prepared to fight.

In the medieval times, both in India and Europe the theoretical instructions gained ground. Even during the English system of education some activities were still considered to be extra-curricular. But during the present century, the whole attitude towards these activities changed. They are now severally named as "curricular activities", "community activities" or simply "activities". They are the essential part of curriculum and the past rigid line of demarcation between the curricular and co-curricular activities is fast disappearing. The Secondary Education Commission has remarked, "They are as integral part of the activities of a school as its curricular work and their proper organisation needs just as much care and thought".

Advantages: Co-curricular activities are certainly useful to students, they help in curricular development. They are also significant in promoting school-community relations.

(a) The co-curricular activities are useful to students in a number of ways:

(i) They provide opportunities for development of new interests. So pursuit of desirable interests gives zest to life and provides an excellent background for profitable use of leisure time. Various activities materially affect children for their vocational choices.

(ii) These activities educate for citizenship through experiences and insight that stress leadership role of students.

(iii) The dictum, "Whom one serves, also loves" applies to both institutions and persons. The pupils can be persuaded to make sacrifices for the school and there by they will learn to love it and will take pride in its success.

(iv) The co-curricular activities provide opportunities for satisfying the gregarious urge of children and youth. The individual identifies himself with the group of his own choice—a debating or dramatic club or the like. He feels no longer as an individual, but a member of the group. The activities like student council, dramatics etc. serve this particular need the best.

(v) These activities encourage moral and spiritual development in the pupils. Education un-inspired by moral and spiritual values is directionless. The child learns through the free community life of games, excursions and the school societies an inner discipline which abides the child as a directing and restraining influence when he is away from the school and even after he has ceased to be a student.

(vi) The co-curricular activities in school provide children a well-rounded social development. They may be instructed how to participate effectively in a group discussion with all good manners.

(vii) These activities go to widen students' contacts. The students nature in their behaviour pattern through Scouting, NCC, Sports Trips, Excursions etc.

(b) The co-curricular activities contribute a lot to improvement of curriculum:

(i) These activities supplement and enrich class room experience. Dramatics, citizenship activities often stem from class room experiences.

(ii) With the help of varied activities, the latest potentialities of pupils can come to the surface. Educational and vocational guidance be given for these to improve quality of pupils. In fact, guidance is inherent in all the co-curricular activities.

(iii) The co-curricular activities motivate class room instruction. That a student is learning best at his level of capability many a student has been kept in school, because of his interest in sports, dramatics, school assembly and the school societies.

(iv) Team work is essential for the smooth functioning of the various organs of the school. Teachers expect co-operation in the class room and the students in turn expect teachers to be interested in the things which interest him such as sports, plays, scouting and other similar activities. The teacher cannot afford to hate students those who are much more interested in co-curricular activities.

(v) Co-curricular activities provide opportunities to the youth in the worthwhile utilisation of their spare time. Leisure time can be converted from a curse into a blessing through these activities.

(vi) The co-curricular activities enable teachers to understand their pupils better. The teacher can get a more complete idea of his student by studying their behaviour in play or other social activities of their own choice. The teacher may see the student who is a "dud" in his history or Mathematics class, may be having the thrill of his life as he plays a match and runs a race.

(vii) Co-curricular activities contribute a lot to the

community. These activities promote better school and community relations. The school and the community can be drawn closer together when the pupils go out on excursions and NCC or Scout Camps.

(viii) When the schools arrange debates, discussions, music concerts where the local pupils may be invited a strong belongingness is drawn between the school and the community.

Defects and Limitations

A number of defects in the organisation of these activities are as follows:

1. *Lack of equipment*: No programme of activities can be successful without proper equipment. Some schools have no playground, no space for indoor activities and no space even for mass-drill especially in over-crowded cities. Some schools lack finances for adequate equipment for sports, exhibitions, dramatics, library work, crafts, hobbies etc. Even some school work lack minimum furniture.
2. *Lack of variety:* Some schools organise a few activities. They do not provide for a sufficient variety of activities to suit the varied interests and abilities of pupils.
3. *Lack of pupil participation*: It is a common observation that majority of pupils do not take part in activities. Perhaps they lack interest and there is no motivation through guidance and encouragement by the staff, may be, the students are overburdened with too much home-work. Some teachers throw the burden of expenses of these activities upon parents. They ask pupils to get from whom costly dresses for dramatics, the musical instruments, hockey sticks and others. Also, the over-crowding in schools is responsible for meagre pupils participation, much emphasis is given on examinations; the pupils are told that these activities do not give credit in the examination.
4. *Defective organisation of the time schedule:* In some schools there is no provision for activities in the daily time

table because these are considered extra to the regular routine. So activities are organised without any pre-planning.

5. *Lack of adequate staff:* Some activities like games and sports, music, scientific hobbies and crafts need specialised staff. A good number of schools do not have PET, music teacher, Science teacher etc. Even schools do not possess a full strength of academic staff and as such, sole burden of organising these activities fall on the existing staff. Naturally the staff members shirk work.
6. *Over-emphasis on academic work:* There is a mad rush for winning distinction of First Division Pass and Scholarships. They publicise their merit even in the press and at the honour-board of the school. In such schools, there is no emphasis on activities. So all extra coaching, private tuition after the school hours in order to achieve better examination results.
7. *Over-emphasis on activities:* In some schools, the case is opposite. Too many activities actually interfere with the regular studies. Almost every day there is a function of one sort or the other, months together are spent on preparations of play or variety show to be shown to the public. Some students who are weak in studies, but are better in games etc. continue to spend all their time in these activities and remain backward as ever.
8. *High work-load of the staff:* There is excessive burden of these activities on staff of under-staffed institutions. To teach more than 40 periods of week and then to organise activities and supervise them daily in the afternoon is an exacting job for a teacher. No extra payment for this over-time work will reward him for the strain of work involved. The only alternative is to expand the staff.

Some Important Co-curricular Activities

1. *The school assembly:* It is a common practice to begin day's work in school with a morning assembly, wherein the entire body of school population assemble for common prayer or talks from teacher. The

morning prayer has become a useful activities in all the schools. Besides prayers of devotion to God, we can have patriotic songs, the flag-songs and songs in praise of our country and nation. There should be a rich variety in the songs, otherwise one prayer song for the whole year will create monotony.

The important objective of the collective gathering of the entire body of pupils is to make announcements regarding the daily work or the school routine. Announcements regarding tournaments, functions, elections, extension lectures, changes in the time table, holidays, changes in the hour of work etc. can conveniently be made at this time. The pupils get an opportunity to feel that the school is an organised group and they develop a sort of community spirit that is not possible if the classes remain isolated from each other and do not meet collectively.

The school assembly provides opportunity to the headmaster and teacher to give talks on various topics of general interest, health and hygiene, reading habits, rules of the road, Panchayati Raj etc.

Advantages

(i) The school assembly works as a unifying force. Students feel the school as an organised group and every student realises that he is part and parcel of the school community.

(ii) Assembly works as a source of inspiration and its experiences widen and deepen students' interests.

(iii) It works as a platform for propagation of commendable work. Outstanding performances and achievements of students in curricular and co-curricular fields get recognised before the entire school. Badges, certificates, cups etc. should be awarded to the winners in the presence of entire school population.

(iv) School assembly serves as a place for developing audience habits. Respects for others' feelings, courtesy towards speakers and guests, sensible applause at the proper time, appreciative attitude are some of the good audience habits that the students develop through school assembly.

(v) Celebration of some of the important national and international days help in broadening the mental horizon of pupils and acquainting them with the life of great scientists, discoverers and statesmen.

(vi) The pupils must come, sit and go in a disciplined manner, gossiping and taking are checked and the atmosphere is made calm and serene. No abusive remarks to students and no unpleasant things are spoken on the scared occasion of total gathering of the school.

2. *Debates and Symposia:* There are literary activities and speech activities; all these go to develop self-expression of students. Debates have important educational value. Through these activities pupils get training in collection of subject-matter, organisation of ideas, speaking effectively and appearing before an audience. The speaker has to control nervousness and stage fright, maintain self-confidence, muster up courage and speak with presence of mind. He gradually learns the art of elocution. His training in oratory, discussion contribute a lot in later year for his public speaking and teaching. Effective speaking is the best qualification of a pupil-leader and through debating and discussion he increases his linguistic ability, enriches his vocabulary and improves his pronunciation. Book works may manage to get a first division in the University examination, but meet of failure at a interview. The importance of debates and other oral activities has been beautifully expressed by McCown.

> "As a developer of intellectual interests and capacities, fluency of expression, clear and discriminating thinking and increased ability to appreciate the important affairs of modern life, good sportsmanship, self-reliance, self-confidence poise any similar desirable qualities, it has few equals in schools".

3. *Dramatics:* Dramatics are the best revenue producers of the entire co-curricular programme. It affords the students opportunities for training in team work. Dramatics possess great possibilities of motivation. A full and inactive class may be transformed into an engaging a busy one, when certain lessons are dramatized under the direction of a skilful instructor. Dramatics help in making the parents interested in school work. Through dramatic historical as well as geographical knowledge of students in increased. Carpentry and other mechanical arts facilitate the work of the construction of stage.

The planning, arranging and setting up the stage should not be made a huge affair such that the students themselves can manage affairs. Entrusting the work of stage to the professionals should be avoided, the teachers should provided necessary instruction and direction. Plays depicting evils of social customs should preferably be chosen. It should be within the capacity of pupils to understand and appreciate. It also should be free from vulgarity and objectionable subject-matter.

4. *Organisation of games and sports:* Games and Sports cater to the all-round development of personality of pupils. Sound mind is ensured in a sound body. Psychologically speaking, play is a biological and social necessity for children. Sports and games ensure the redirection of surplus of energy of adolescents to fruitful channels. It is said that play is the most useful leisure time activity of the adolescents. It is a training for future. In the absence of opportunities for play the pupils are forced to frequent cinemas, clubs, hotels cafeteria, circus and theatres. Good sportsmen have promising future to work. So play ground is said to be the "uncovered school" and the "cradle of democracy".

The greatest lacuna in the present educational set-up in the country is the conspicuous absence of facilities and opportunities for games and athletics. In many schools, there are no proper play fields. Secondary Education Commission painfully observes the absence of play fields and suggests that the municipal parks or any open apace available in the neighbourhood should be utilised by the school.

Organisation of games and sports should be there in each and every school as follows:

(i) Opportunity should be provided for every pupil in the school.
(ii) A time-schedule should be prepared for each of the games and sports available in the school. Small groups and teams should be formed. Various periods may be allotted to different groups.
(iii) Arrangements should be made that every pupils gets necessary equipment from the school. Poor students should not be expected to undergo expense for sports materials.
(iv) Necessary guidance and coaching may be provided through physical education instructors.

(v) A good variety of games must be introduced. Besides Football, Hockey, Cricket, indigenous games like "Kabbadi", "Khokho" and "Tug-O-War" should be introduced in schools. Some very common and popular country games prevalent in the locality may be there in the school. Simple athletics like high jump, long jump, discus throw, javelin throw, putting the shot, hurdles race and the like which do not require much space as playground should be practised.

(vi) Games suitable for girls should be introduced in girl schools and in co-education school.

(vii) The inter-school contest should not be given undue importance, sometimes, mutual jealousies spring forth. This should be avoided under circumstances.

5. *Boy Scouting and Girl Guiding:* Scouting is a multipurpose activity relating to pupils from 11 to 18. Every Scout makes a solemn pledge to obey the Scout Laws. Thus he is trained to have best personality traits. The Boy Scouts make the promise to obey the Scout laws, learn the use of ropes and sticks, learn first aid and social services, organise camp fires, organise picnics and outings. The activities of Girl Guides includes cooking, nursing, first aid, singing dancing, games, drill and social service.

Advantages of Scouting and Girl Guiding are numerous:

(i) It is an open secret that an average student shirks work. But scouting promotes health and physical well-being of pupils through a network of organised physical activities.

(ii) It contributes to mental health of adolescents through pleasing and cheerful tasks they are engaged in.

(iii) It appeals to the impulses and urges of the adolescents and provides a fruitful channel for the expression of their tendencies. It sublimates instincts of curiosity, assertiveness and gregariousness.

(iv) It promotes the spirit of adventure through camping life and outdoor life.

(v) Scouting is a social training. Through camp life and co-operative activities, it teaches ideals of citizenship, mutual helps, co-operation, mutual toleration, fellow-feeling, compassion of all suffers and self-sacrifice for the community. A Scout is trained to render all types of social services i.e. cleanliness of surroundings, voluntary labour, village uplifts, anti-malaria work, adult literacy work, first aid, nursing and service in fairs and exhibitions. Scouting emphasises manual work and dignity of labour, a very important social virtue.

(vi) A true Scout who obeys ten laws can never be indisciplined. Obviously if scouting is run at right lines, the atmosphere in the secondary schools is bound to be congenial and disciplined.

6. *Field trips and excursions:* Arrangement of educational field tours and excursions is considered now as an essential part of school programmes. By moving outdoors, the pupils get concrete information and enrich their personal experience. The mental horizon of pupils gets widened. Again,' during the course of trip all arrangements of travelling, boarding and lodging are made by pupils. This provides a practical training to develop the qualities of initiative, resourcefulness and self-confidence.

The educational trips can be of varied interests. Visits to museums, forts, temples, caves, forests, mountains, lakes, valleys, canals and corn fields help in supplementing the teaching of social studies, history, geography etc. Excursion to Red Fort, Agra Fort, Taj Mahal, Elora and Ajanta brings reality, clarity and vividness to the "dead matter" of history. Visits to industrial establishments, factories, laboratories etc. are very helpful to the students taking up science.

As per organisation of Field Trips and Excursions it is very necessary that it should be properly planned to achieve the maximum benefit from excursion. It must be wisely be conceived, ably conducted and intelligently evaluated. The teacher in-charge should posses complete information regarding the place of visit. He must impart all the valuable knowledge to the pupils. The railway reservation of accommodation for entire route of movement and lodging at each place of stay should be thoroughly planned before-hand. All haste should be avoided. The entire work must be divided among the workers and group-leaders. Proper budgeting should be done and economy must be observed. Recreational activities like singing, story-telling, photography should be organised side by side. Lastly care must be taken for maintenance of perfect discipline in the entire course of excursion.

7. *NCC and ACC:* The values of military training is very great. In almost all countries of the West regular military training to the young has become a regular feature of the national life. In an emergency or critical situation when the security of the people is in danger, the students come forward to defend the country. The NCC in India is going to fulfil the long-felt military needs of the students.

The Secondary Education Commission has suggested that the recruitment and the training of NCC, should receive great attention from the Defence Department. The National Cadet Corps consists of three divisions (a) Junior Divisions in the High Schools and the Public Schools. It comprises three Units of Army, Navy and Air Force. (b) In Colleges Senior Division of NCC functions. (c) Girls Division Unit is gradually becoming popular.

The Government of India have setup an organisation called the Auxiliary Cadet Corps with "Service to the Country (DESH SEVA)" as its motto.

8. *Social Service:* Some form of social and national service should be made as integral part of education at all stages. This should be done by students' participation in the programmes of community living on the school campus and of community development of national reconstruction.

There are various opportunities for community work in the class room on the school campus and in the school hostels. In many schools, the students undertake cleaning the school rooms and school premises, levelling the playground, preparing and maintaining a school garden polishing the furniture, whitewashing the walls and painting the doors and windows.

A well-trained teacher, who maintains good relations with the local community can easily find appropriate situations connected with public sanitation. The school children can help to the old and sick in simple village improvement projects. At the secondary stage, the children are more mature and it is possible to organise programmes of community service at a higher level.

It is no easy task to organise an effective programme of social service for all secondary schools in the country. To begin with some selected schools of high-quality may organise the National Service Programme on a voluntary basis. The training schools and colleges may take the lead in this regard.

9. *Work Experience:* The Education Commission (1964-66) writes "Work-experience, which involves participation in some modern form of productive work under conditions approximating to those found in real life situation should be introduced as an integral part of education at all stages. It will provide a much-needed corrective to the extremely academic and bookish character of present school education."

In lower classes of primary schools, work-experience may begin as simple handwork, the objective being to train children to make use of their hands and thereby help their intellectual and emotional growth. Paper cutting, cardboard cutting and folding, clay modelling, spinning, simple planting indoors or on plots, kitchen gardening etc.

In upper primary schools, cane and bamboo work, leather work, pottery, needle work, weaving, gardening, model making, works on the farms etc. should be the chief work experience of the pupils. In the senior classes it may take the form of learning a craft, which develops technical thinking and creative capacities in the pupils. Even here some work-experience can be provided in real life situation as work on the farms at the time of sowing and harvesting.

It is proposed that a workshop would be attached to every school OT group of secondary schools in a phased programme spread over the next ten years. Work-experience at the Lower Secondary Stage can take the form of workshop training. Here these experience will include book work, simple metal work, basket work, leather work, soap making, tanning, weaving, electric repairs, cookery, classroom decoration, book binding, tailoring, toy making, wood carving, simple form of mechanics, animal care, crop care, care for the soil and the like.

Many of these activities listed above would be continued, but the emphasis would shift to actual work-experience in industrial or commercial concerns or on farms. Always, the activities would be oriented towards productive work.

The Kothari Commission observes, "The concept of work-experience is closely related to the philosophy underlying basis education. The programme of basic education did involve work-experience for all children in the primary school, though the activities, proposed were concerned with the indigenous crafts and the village employment patterns."

A beginning should be made immediately in some selected schools. It should be declared objective of state policy to increase the facilities for work-experience in industry and agriculture. A programme of modernisation or a forward look should be built into the schedule of work in school. So the possible problem of training of teachers in this direction, provision of necessary facilities including supply of equipment and the progressive extension of the programme to all the schools should be very carefully tackled.

10. *Hobbies: Hobby is* a pleasureful engagement in work at the time of leisure. It is a work of sweet will. So hobby is a social necessity in the modern times. The present machine age has placed enough leisure time at the disposal of man. Every prudent and a modern adult must utilise leisure time fruitfully. This is only possible by busying oneself in a hobby. But adult age is too late for the selection of a hobby. The best time for such selection is the childhood. Hobbies represent important past time of the pupils and these help them in promotion of discipline with pleasure.

The hobbies have the following educative values:

(i) These help in the development of innate powers.
(ii) These are the best substitutes of play at the adolescent and adult level.
(iii) These provide relief from dull and dreary work of the school.
(iv) These have recreational and aesthetic value.
(v) These would solve the problem of spending leisure hours.
(vi) To some these help in preparing for vocations like painting and photography which may give economic benefit also.

Individuals differ in their interest, aptitude, attitude, ability, tastes and the like. So pupils are interested in various types of hobbies. The chief types of hobbies for school children may be categorised as follows:

(i) *Collection:* Collecting stamps, seeds, leaves, flowers, feathers, stones, fossils, match-boxes, pictures, cartoons, coins etc.

(ii) *Artistic Hobbies:* Like include drawing, painting, clay modelling, book-binding, toy-making, sculpture designing, embroidery, preparing cartoons etc.

(iii) *Scientific Hobbies:* Like preparing soap and candle, radio repairing, photography, preparing improvised scientific apparatus, preparing electrical appliances of daily use etc.

(iv) *Social Hobbies:* Like playing chess, attending clubs, making correspondence with pen friends etc.

(v) *Library Hobbies:* Like writing small poems, short stories etc.

(vi) *Craft Hobbies*: Like spinning, weaving, kitchen-gardening, leather work, basket making, tailoring knitting etc.

References

Adams, Harold P. and Dickey, F.G. *Supervision for better Schools*, New Delhi, Eurasia Publishing House Pvt. Ltd., 1966.

Agarwal, J.C., *Educational Administration School, Organisation & Supervision,* New Delhi, Arya Book Depot, 1967.

Aggarwal, J.C., *Modern Indian Education*, Delhi, Shipra Publications, 2010.

Agrawal, Rashmi, *Educational Technology, Management and Evaluation*, Delhi, Shipra Publications, 2010.

Barr, A.S. Burton, W. H. and Brueckner, L.J., *Supervision,* New York Appleton-Century Crofts Inc. 1947.

Best, John W., *Research in Education,* New Delhi Prentice Hall of India Pvt. Ltd. 1963.

Brown, E.J., *Educational Sociology, New York.* Prentice Hall, 1962.

Brown, M. *Effective Supervision,* New York, Macmillan and Co. 1956.

Brubacher, J.S., *A History of the Problems of Education,* New York Mc. Grew Hill Book Co. 1947.

Burton, William H. *et al. Supervision, A Social Process,* Appliton Century Crofts 1955.

Das, K.K, and Das, K.B. (Mrs.), *School Administration & Health Education,* Cuttack Scientific Book Depot, 1976.

Dash, S.C. and Parhi, J.N., *The Study of the Methods of Inspection of Primary Schools in Orissa* 1966, S.I.E. Bhubaneswar.

Dash, S.C., *Utkalmani Gopabandhu Dash,* Cuttack, Gopabandhu Press, 1980.

Dewey, J., *Democracy and Education,* New York, Macmillan & Co., 1957.

Dewey, J., *Experience and Education,* New York, Macmillan & Co., 1952.

Dewey, J., *School and Society,* New York, Macmillan & Co., 1932.

Elsbree, W.S., McNally H.J., *Elementary School Administration* Eurasia Publishing House Pvt. Ltd., New Delhi 1964.

Gupta, S., Aggarwal, J.C., *School Management*, Delhi, Shipra Publications, 2007.

Hagman, H.L., *Administration of Elementary Schools,* New York.

Harris, Chester, W., *Encyclopaedia of Educational Research,* New York, The Macmillan Co. 1960.

Havinghurst, R.J., *Developmental Tasks and Education,* Longmans, London, 1949.

Indian Institute of Public Administration, *The Journal of Public Administration* Vol. 1 No. l, 1954.

Jain, M.K. and Aggarwal, J.C., *Encyclopedia of Education,* 6 Vols., Delhi, Shipra Publications, 2010.

Josephine, Yazali, *School Resource Planning and Management*, Delhi, Shipra Publications, 2005.

Kanungo, G.B., *Gopabandhu's Educational, Experiment at Satyabadi, Souvenir, 10th Conference.* Indian Association of Teacher Education, Bhubaneswar, 1967.

Katz, Joseph. *Elementary Education in Canada,* New York, McGraw Hill Co. Canada Ltd. 1961

Kearney, Nolan C., *Elementary School Objectives.*

Kochhar, S.K., *Secondary School Administration.* New Delhi Sterling Publishers Pvt. Ltd. 1981.

Kripalani, J.B., *The Latest Fad,* Sevagram, Wardha Hindustani Talim Sangh, 1954.

Miahra, C.S., *Satyabadire satabarsa* (In Oriya) Cuttack Students Store, Cuttack, 1966.

Mohanty J., *Foundation of Education,* Takshyashila, Cuttack.

Mohanty, J. "A Study of Inspection Reports of Primary Schools" *Research Bulletin,* SIE Maharashtra, Puna March, 1973.

Mohanty, J. *Educational Administration Inspection and Supervision,* Vidyapuri, 1981.

Mohanty, J., *Educational Technology & Communications,* Cuttack, Nalanda, 1980.

Mohanty, J., *Indian Education in the Emerging Society,* New Delhi, Sterling Publishers Pvt. Ltd. 1982.

Mukerji, S.N. (Ed.) *Administration of Education in India,* Baroda, Acharya Book Depot, 1968.

Mukherjee, S.N., *History of Education in India.* Modern period, Boroda, Archya Book Depot, 1966.

Mukherjee, V., *Problems of Administration of Education in India,* Allahabad Kitab Mahal, 1960.

Mukhopadhyay, Marmar, *Ancient Indian Education*, New Delhi, Shipra Publications, 2010.

Naik, J.P., A paper on "*Role and function of the State Institute of Education*" presented in the Workshop of Principles and Vice-Principals, New Delhi, 1964.

Nair, T.K.D., *School Planning and Management: A Democratic Approach*, Delhi, Shipra Publications, 2004.

Naik, J.P., *Educational Planning in India.* Bombay, Allied Publishers Pvt. Ltd. 1965.

Narula, M., *Quality in School Education: Secondary Education & Education Board*, New Delhi, NUEPA, 2010.

NCERT, New Delhi, *The Indian Yearbook of Education,* 1964, "Elementary Education."

NCERT, Report of the Study Group on Supervision and Inspection, 1969.

Neagley, Ross J. and Evans, N. Dean, *Handbook for Effective Supervision of Instruction,* London, Prentice Hall, 1961.

Nunn, T.P., *Education, Its Data and First Principles,* London, Edward Arnold & Co., 1930.

Nurullah, S. and Naik J.P., *A Students' History of Education in India,* The Macmillan Company of India Pvt. Ltd. 1971.

Otto, Henery J., *Principles of Elementary Education,* New York Holt Rinchart and Winston, 1955.

Patel, M.S., *Educational Philosophy of Mahatma Gandhi* Ahmadabad, Navajeeban Publishing House, 1953.

Planning Commission, Government of India, *Educational Planning, Administration and Evaluation in the Fourth Plan,* 1968.

Rai, B.C., *Problems of Indian Education, Lucknow,* Prakashan Kendra, New Buildings, Ahmadabad, 1975.

Reburn, W.M., *The Organisation of Schools,* London, Oxford University Press, 1970.

Ross, J., *Ground-work of Educational Theory,* London George H. Harrap, 1942.

Rusk, R.R., *The Doctrines of Great Educators,* London, Macmillan, 1962.

Safaya R.N. & Shaida, B.D., *School Administration & Organisation* Delhi, Dhanpat Rai & Sons, 1980.

Safaya, R.N., *Current Problems in Indian Education* Delhi-Jullunder, Dhanpat Rai & Sons, 1976.

Saiyadain, K.G. *Compulsory Education in India,* Delhi, UNESCO, 1952.

Satpathy, N., *He Sathi, He Sarathi,* Cuttack, J. Mahapatra & Co, Chhatrasathi Press, 1976.

Sears, J.B., *Public School Administration,* New York, Ronald Press.

Sears, J.B., *The Nature of the Administrative Process,* New York, McGraw Hill Book Co., 1950.

Siqueira. T.N., *Modern Indian Education,* London, Oxford University Press, 1960,

Suryarao, B., *Current Problems in Indian Education,* Guntur, Srinibas Printers, 1970.

Tilak, Jandhyala B.G., *Financing of Secondary Education in India*, New Delhi, NUEPA–Shipra, 2008.

Tyagi, Rajvir Singh, *Administration & Management in School Education*, New Delhi, Shipra Publications, 2010.

Venkataswamy, N., *A Study of the Work of Supervisors,* S.I.E. Andhra Pradesh.

Whetney, F.W., *The Elements of Research, Bombay,* Asia Pub. House, 1961.

Whitehead, A.N., *The Aims of Education & other Essays.* New York, Mentore Books, 1957.